THE SCHOOL MENTOR'S GUIDE

Sara Miller McCune founded SAGE Publishing in 1965 to support the dissemination of usable knowledge and educate a global community. SAGE publishes more than 1000 journals and over 800 new books each year, spanning a wide range of subject areas. Our growing selection of library products includes archives, data, case studies and video. SAGE remains majority owned by our founder and after her lifetime will become owned by a charitable trust that secures the company's continued independence.

Los Angeles | London | New Delhi | Singapore | Washington DC | Melbourne

THE SCHOOL MENTOR'S GUIDE

HOW TO MENTOR NEW & BEGINNING TEACHERS

COLIN HOWARD, JOY CARROLL
JANE OWENS & DÉBORAH LANGSTON

Learning Matters
A SAGE Publishing Company
1 Oliver's Yard
55 City Road
London EC1Y 1SP

SAGE Publications Inc.
2455 Teller Road
Thousand Oaks, California 91320

SAGE Publications India Pvt Ltd
B 1/I 1 Mohan Cooperative Industrial Area
Mathura Road
New Delhi 110 044

SAGE Publications Asia-Pacific Pte Ltd
3 Church Street
#10-04 Samsung Hub
Singapore 049483

Editor: Amy Thornton
Senior project editor: Chris Marke
Project management: Deer Park Productions
Marketing manager: Lorna Patkai
Cover design: Wendy Scott
Typeset by: C&M Digitals (P) Ltd, Chennai, India
Printed in the UK

Library of Congress Control Number: 2019954895

British Library Cataloguing in Publication Data

A catalogue record for this book is available from the
British Library

ISBN 978-1-5264-9452-8
ISBN 978-1-5264-9451-1 (pbk)

At SAGE we take sustainability seriously. Most of our products are printed in the UK using responsibly sourced
papers and boards. When we print overseas we ensure sustainable papers are used as measured by the
PREPS grading system. We undertake an annual audit to monitor our sustainability.

CONTENTS

ABOUT THE AUTHORS

Colin Howard is an Associate Primary Lecturer in Initial Teacher Education (ITT) at the University of Worcester. He has been involved in primary education for over 24 years of which 14 years has been as a successful head teacher in both small village and large primary school settings. He has a strong research interest which includes primary science, aspects of professional practice and teachers' professional identity. He is a SIAMS inspector of the Diocese of Hereford.

Deborah Langston is a Principal Lecturer in Initial Teacher Education (ITT) at the University of Worcester. She is a member of the Primary management team and is Primary Partnership Lead. With responsibility for NQT support, Deborah enjoys close links with former students. Prior to joining the university Deborah worked for 25 years in a wide variety of school settings. She was a class-based teaching deputy head teacher for three years and a successful head teacher at a school in Worcestershire for 11 years during which time she also took the roles of SENCo and Safeguarding lead. Research interests include inclusion, the importance and impact of teamwork, leadership and teacher efficacy.

Jane Owens is a Senior Lecturer in Education at the University of Worcester, where she is module lead for the MA Education mentoring and coaching modules. In addition to this part-time lecturing role, Jane is an MA Coaching Dissertation Supervisor with the University of Warwick's Centre for Lifelong Learning and is a Skills Coach/Placement Tutor at Aston University. She also runs her own limited company through which she delivers coaching, training and research assignments. Prior to this, Jane worked as a Senior Consultant within an economic consultancy firm and, before that, worked within local authority careers services and education business partnerships.

Joy Carroll is a Senior Lecturer in Primary Initial Teacher Education (ITE) at the University of Worcester. She teaches on the undergraduate and post-graduate courses and is Partnership Placement Manager. Before moving into ITE she worked as an assistant head teacher and a class teacher and in primary schools in London, Hereford, Worcester and Stafford and was the manager of a private nursery school. Following this, Joy worked as an advisor within the area of school workforce in a local authority, working closely with schools on deployment of support staff. She is currently working on doctoral research into how schools and universities work in partnership to support ITE.

1

iNTRODUCTiON: THE PROFESSiONAL ROLE OF A TEACHER MENTOR

CHAPTER OBJECTiVES

By the end of this chapter you should be aware of:

- a need for high-quality school mentors for trainees and early career teachers
- how mentoring may be defined
- how individuals may be encouraged to take on the role of mentoring
- the role that mentoring plays in developing and establishing outstanding practice in trainee and early career teachers
- the need for a clear set of Mentor Standards to support its provision and development in schools alongside initial teacher training (ITT) institutions students and their training.

iNTRODUCTiON

This chapter will outline the current theory and research underpinning the mentoring of trainee and early career teachers in schools. It will establish the need for ITT and for school partners to provide high-quality mentor support for individuals. This chapter also will promote a need for training to be extended to those teachers who provide such invaluable mentoring provision within schools.

THE PROFESSiONAL ROLE OF THE MENTOR

For many individuals the notion of becoming a teacher and starting on a teacher training course may be underpinned by what often is described as a calling (Bullough and Hall-Kenyon, 2012) – an altruistic wish to empower both children and young adults to achieve their best in schools. For researchers such as Huberman (1993) and Day et al. (2007) the drive to teach may be promoted by their hope of providing a rewarding chance to work with children and young people, thus encouraging their progress. For others, such a drive to teach may be linked to other more personal motives such as to emulate an individual's teaching family history.

For many/all trainee teachers such a wish to teach will be rooted in a fundamental desire to enable children and young people to succeed academically, socially and emotionally. This, no doubt, will be rooted in the hope of enabling such individuals to make a positive contribution to society. Alongside such a desire for teachers to promote personal development in others there may also be a wish to support and nurture individuals who wish to choose a career in education. For many teachers this will include mentoring trainee teachers and early career teachers who are new to the profession. This will no doubt be so that they can embark upon a long and successful teaching career.

JOURNEY iNTO TEACHiNG

For numerous trainee teachers their route to achieving qualified teacher status (QTS) will be varied. For some it will be through the more traditional ITT programmes such as a Post-Graduate Certificate in Education (PGCE) whilst for others it will be through newer school-based pathways such as Teach First. As the National Audit Office (2016, p.16) suggests, however, though in England there may be a variety of pathways taken in order to gain QTS, the majority of such routes being university led. This must be seen against a backdrop of a move towards more school-centred training.

The majority of university-based routes to QTS may be achieved through more traditional courses which include programmes such as a three-year Bachelor of Arts Honours Degree with QTS or a one-year PGCE with QTS. QTS may also be achieved by the more recently established school-based training programmes such as the Post-Graduate Teaching Apprenticeship, School Direct or Teach First, or through school-centred initial teacher training (SCITT) programmes (the latter often being run by schools or groups of schools). The majority of these more recently established routes will be based outside a university campus though they will have formed close working links or partnerships with a university, thus allowing the trainee teachers to gain a PGCE with an award of QTS status.

To some extent this myriad of school-based programmes has been spawned against an ideological background where teaching may be seen as a craft learned as part of an apprenticeship-based model of training (Gove, 2010). However, no matter the route taken to achieve QTS, all such programmes will be underpinned by a desire to promote outstanding teaching as outlined by the Teachers' Standards (DfE, 2011). Once graduated, and in receipt of QTS, a trainee teacher's journey will start by them becoming an 'early career teacher'. This term encapsulates the journey from gaining QTS to what is known as being a newly qualified teacher (NQT) and then to becoming a recently qualified teacher (RQT). Embedded within the current draft of an Early Career Framework (ECF) by the Department of Education (DfE, 2019), an early career teacher's journey of learning will continue with a two-year programme of structured training and development. This is currently planned to be rolled out nationally from September 2021 with a desire not only to support the needs of early career teachers, but also, importantly, to enable them to be successful as they join the teaching profession.

For fledgling teachers, both as a trainee and during their early career, the Teaching Schools Council (2016) alongside DfE (2019) suggest that mentoring will play a significant role in supporting trainees and accredited teachers in the early stages of their careers; early career teachers are currently being supported by a designated mentor throughout what is known as their induction year (DfE, 2018b). The Department of Education suggests that during a teacher's induction it will be essential that early career teachers are given the opportunity to: 'develop the knowledge, practices and working habits that set them up for a fulfilling and successful career in teaching' (DfE, 2019, p.4). For the DfE (2019, p.4) teachers new to the profession are seen as the basis of our future educational system and as such:

> *teachers deserve high quality support throughout their careers, particularly in those first years of teaching when the learning curve is steepest … teachers in the first years of their career require high quality, structured support in order to begin the journey towards becoming an expert.*

It is important to recognise, however, that such teacher support arrangements may not be found exclusively within school mentor/mentee relationships. They may extend to teachers identifying their own informal support networks. These may also provide fledging professionals with advice and support through what can be seen as a difficult period of a teacher's career. As teachers progress further into their careers, such support networks may be found to extend to other teachers/senior leaders who are able to provide informal mentoring advice. Such informal networks may play an important role in order for them to achieve future school roles such as being a subject lead or co-ordinator or middle leader/ head teacher.

The transition from early career teacher to qualified professional teacher is not without its highs and lows. This includes, for example, the positive rewards of supporting children to succeed academically and socially alongside more challenging issues, with some of these causing stresses and strains for a developing professional. For example, these may include dealing with teacher workload or disruptive behaviours in the classroom. Such items, as reported by a recent ATL survey (ATL Media Office, 2017), have resulted in three-quarters of trainee and NQTs considering leaving the teaching profession. Given such findings, and the realities of being part of the teaching profession, it would seem vital that they are successfully inducted and supported into their new teaching role by outstanding school mentors. It will be a mentor's listening and interpersonal skills, alongside their emotional support, which will no doubt support their mentees, as trainee and early career teachers, to face the stresses and strains within their developing professional career thus aiding their retention (Gardiner and Weisling, 2018). Effective mentors may also support such professionals to become proficient and confident in their daily working lives and to become resilient so as to withstand the trials and tribulations of being part of the teaching profession. The desire to provide a coherent package of support for early career teachers has seen the drafting of the ECF by the Department of Education (DfE, 2019). Such a document clearly signals the priority of the relationship that school mentors may play in supporting early career teachers, and includes a suggestion that time should be funded, so that mentors can support such individuals, alongside fully funded mentor training (DfE, 2019). This suggestion is underpinned by the notion of developing mentors who will seek to support, challenge, feedback and critique to enable teachers' achievement of professional standards.

TOWARDS DEFINING MENTORING

For many, mentoring may be seen as a 'dynamic process' (Gardiner and Weisling, 2018, p.331) as well as a complex role, especially given the knowledge and interpersonal skills needed to undertake such a position. Researchers such as Aspfors and Fransson (2015, p.77) even suggest that mentoring may be seen as a: 'a profession within the teaching profession'. Thus it is important that, before commencing any book relating to mentoring, that there should be an unpicking of what is a complex phenomenon. As Aspfors and Fransson (2015) rightly conclude, mentoring and mentor education cannot be studied fully without questioning how it may be understood and defined. An analysis of this concept may also serve to share a common understanding of what is, at the very least, a complex, situated, layered and demanding role (Gardiner and

Weisling, 2018). Many researchers, for example Hobson and Malderez (2013) and Hobson et al. (2009), have sought to define this concept. However, as Gardiner and Weisling (2018, p.338) suggest: 'there is no agreed-upon definition of mentoring or its purpose'.

Clearly mentoring is multifaceted in nature. For some researchers there is a suggestion that mentoring may be identified in terms of 'coaching, training and guiding' (Izadinia, 2016, p.399). For others it may be in terms of its context, purpose, theoretical approaches, duration and intensity (Aspfors and Fransson, 2015, p.76). Given such variance it is inevitable that, when attempting to make a universal definition, such a notion may be seen as problematic (Aspfors and Fransson, 2015). However as Roberts (2000, p.145) indicates, without a clear definition of mentoring: 'how may we ever know that we are talking about the same thing?'.

Early considerations of this concept, as Lindgren (2007) suggests, may be found in Greek mythology, with the role of mentor described as being 'an adviser, teacher and friend' (Lindgren, 2007, p.252). More recently a drive to define and interpret mentoring has led to researchers such as Roberts (2000) and Aspfors and Fransson (2015) linking the term to a process. For Hobson and Malderez (2013, p.90) such a process entails the 'educator' providing suitable opportunities for a mentee's professional learning.

However by examining what may be seen as many and varied definitions for this concept, and considering the remit of this book, its authors wish to adopt a definition of mentoring as outlined within *The National Standards for School-Based Initial Teacher Training (ITT) Mentors* (Teaching Schools Council, 2016, p.7) which defines a mentor as:

> *a suitably-experienced teacher who has formal responsibility to work collaboratively within the ITT partnership to help ensure the trainee receives the highest-quality training.*

A MENTOR'S ROLE

Whilst such a definition may, by its very nature, tell us some things about a mentor's role (in so far as they will be working with the ITT partnership and ensuring highest-quality training for the trainee teacher(s) they support) it does not tell us anything about how they will carry out their mentoring role nor what is required for their efforts to be effective. Limited research also serves to cloud what constitutes the route taken from being an experienced teacher to a mentor beginning on their journey of that of an experienced mentor. What is clear, however, is that mentor teachers will, as Gardiner and Weisling suggest, face many challenges developing and sustaining relationships (Gardiner and Weisling, 2018). It is therefore crucial that, throughout this book, there should be an examination of the role of a mentor and mentor/mentee relationship alongside the skills, knowledge and attitudes needed to be successful in this role.

Help to define the remit of a school-based mentor can, however, be found in *The National Standards for School-Based Initial Teacher Training (ITT) Mentors* (Teaching Schools Council, 2016, p.8) which contains a short section on 'the role of the mentor'. This indicates that the mentor should:

- understand the course structure

- know trainees are required to meet the Teachers' Standards

- prioritise meetings and discussions with a trainee

- monitor the trainee's performance

- help to develop the trainee's teaching practice and their effective classroom management strategies

- keep their own subject knowledge up to date

- signpost trainees to other sources of expertise and knowledge.

Though such a list provides much needed detail about a mentor's role, it is still not exactly clear what the extent and complexity of such a role is. For researchers, such as Roberts (2000, pp.151–8), mentoring is a process which may include attributes such as:

- an active relationship

- a helping process

- a teaching–learning process

- reflective practice

- a career and personal development process

- a formalised process

- a role constructed by or for a mentor (in response to expectations).

Roberts (2000, p.158) also goes on to outline attributes of mentoring which, though not essential, may include:

- role modelling

- sponsoring (when older people within an organisation take a lesser developed individual 'under their wing')

- coaching.

For the purpose of this book, and in order to summarise what is a complex concept – i.e. effective mentoring – we have chosen two quotes that we believe offer insight into what effective mentoring may prove to be.

Firstly:

> *mentoring is a structured, sustained process for supporting professional learners through significant career transitions and mentors are experienced colleagues with knowledge of the requirements of the role.* (CUREE, 2005, p.3)

And mentoring is:

> *a long term relationship that meets a development need, offered by a senior or more experienced individual to a junior or less experienced individual where the less experienced individual receives guidance, advice and support to help their development.* (Passmore et al, 2017, p.8)

Such quotes may provide the reader with a starting point to help consider what effective mentoring may be. These quotes also create an image of a caring and supportive (yet challenging) professional relationship between a mentor and mentee and provide an important counterbalance to what appears to be taking place in some schools, with recent research from the DfE (2018a, p.8) noting:

> *while mentoring emerges in a positive light, there is some evidence of a perception that formal conversations with mentors are primarily evaluative, with a lesser or absent developmental function.*

As this chapter progresses, it seeks to explore the varying perspectives on mentors and mentoring practice. It will explore the role of an effective mentor and consider the idea that it may not be solely linked to that of an individual's persona. It will also consider the role of mentor's preparedness for their roles. Such a notion is set against a backdrop of individuals who so often are reported to be ill-prepared and trained, rendering them unable to be successful and effective in their duties.

This book also examines, in greater detail, skills, knowledge and attitudes needed to support, develop and challenge trainee and early career teachers and to help them become outstanding practitioners.

KEY REFLECTIONS

- How would you define the role of a mentor?
- What qualities, skills and attitudes are required to be a successful mentor?

SCHOOL-BASED MENTORING

Since the early 1980s, school-based mentoring has become increasingly prominent in supporting trainee teachers alongside early career teachers both nationally and internationally (Hobson et al., 2009; Hobson and Malderez, 2013; Lindgren 2007; Marable and Raimondi, 2007). This increased focus is attributed to many issues including the factors outlined by Hobson et al. (2009) and Roehrig et al. (2008). These include:

- supporting the increased supply of teachers into the profession via a range of routes to gain teacher training certification

- reducing the challenges encountered by new teachers

- promoting the retention of those new to the profession

- a means of rewarding and retaining those most capable of teaching.

For researchers such as Hobson et al. (2009, p.208) this drive towards the increased significance of mentoring may also be linked to an historic need to: 'overcome the theory–practice dualism found to be endemic to traditional, higher education institutions (HEI) or college based programmes' (Hobson et al., 2009, p.208).

A school-based mentoring approach to teacher training is not without its critics. Sceptics suggest that this approach can be attributed to a wider move towards employment-based teacher training, alongside a desire to 'de-intellectualise the critical preparation' (Hobson et al., 2009, p.208).

Despite such viewpoints, and however you wish to view the reasoning behind the drive and need for mentoring of trainees in schools, what would seem important is a trainee's needs to manage and be trained to be well prepared for this professional role. This will be against many challenges they will face in their jobs such as behaviour management, assessment and planning (Roehrig et al., 2008). Further to this, one cannot escape the influence that mentor/trainee relationships may have upon the construction of a teacher's professional identity in a negative or positive way (Izadinia, 2016). Researchers such as Day el al. (2007, p.102) suggest teacher identity should be seen in terms of: 'how teachers define themselves to themselves and others'. In turn, this construction of identity plays a significant role in a teacher's decision-making (Izadinia, 2016).

As Izadinia (2016) suggests, such social relationships (i.e. open and honest relationships) with significant others during their training (i.e. their mentor) will not only have a significant impact upon a teacher's identity but also upon how mentors interact with teachers. Such relationships will, in turn, be influenced by a teacher's own experiences of school life. They may also be influenced by their own beliefs about what it may be to be a teacher (Flores and Day, 2006), with a teacher's own construction of professional identity being seen to ebb and flow in terms of their multiple identities (i.e. 'personal, professional and situated/socially located') over their career phases (Day et al., 2007, p.106).

It is also important to recognise the presence of a 'close emotional connection' between the trainees and mentor (Izadinia, 2016, p.399) and the role that such a relationship can play in not only shaping a trainee's future professional identity but also in proffering up 'professional knowledge, technical support and help to develop their own teaching style' to such individuals (Izadinia, 2016, p.389). Such a mentor/mentee relationship must also be seen to promote an ever-increasing aspect of a trainee/early career teacher's personal support in terms of their personal and professional well-being. This support is vital given the stresses and strains they are likely to face in their chosen, and demanding, career.

For some researchers however, such as Hobson and Malderez (2013, pp.92–3), mentoring is not without its negative influences upon those new to the profession. For example, this may include actions which can:

> stunt beginner teachers' professional learning and growth … [and] … has damaged beginning teachers' self-esteem, caused anxiety and stress and contributed to mentees' decisions to leave the profession.

It is also important to recognise that such a mentee/mentor relationship should not simply be characterised by the feeling that the inculcation of learning is from mentor to mentee. For some researchers, including Aspfors and Fransson (2015), mentors can learn from early career teachers in terms of new perspectives and current knowledge relating to the teaching profession. Bressman et al. (2018, p.164) suggest it can allow teachers to 'experiment with creative solutions to problems in a safe and supportive environment', as well as become more 'intentional in their teaching'. In addition to this, such a relationship may lead to a teacher being afforded an opportunity to develop their interpersonal skills so as to better read and engage with their mentee. For some teachers, engaging in the mentoring processes may be seen as reflective, thus allowing teachers to reconsider and therefore re-evaluate their own current practice.

Despite, the significance of the mentor/mentee teacher relationship it seems ironic that for many school mentors such a role may have developed by chance when another mentor leaves the school. A new mentor is needed and the post may be allocated through seniority of professional practice or through discussion with their head teacher (perhaps during a performance management conversation). For others, this role may have come about by a teacher being asked (or told) to mentor a trainee teacher. As Hobson and Malderez (2013, p.97) suggest, many schools:

> do not employ rigorous methods of mentor selection based upon clear criteria, including aptitude for the role based on prior experience and perceived characteristics and expertise, and a willingness to assume it.

Such factors may, as Hobson and Malderez (2013, p.98) suggest, lead to mentors being ill-suited, insufficiently committed and 'judgementoring' (with methods inappropriate to professional development and learning), as well as being unfamiliar with university-based course requirements and content.

CASE STUDY: DEBORAH

> Deborah has been working at her school for a few years and the head teacher is aware she is ambitious. Since there are no senior management opportunities currently available the head teacher has asked Deborah if she would like to become a mentor for trainee teachers in school. The head teacher is aware this will allow Deborah to gain middle leader experience given the current lack of opportunities for this in her setting. It will allow her to gain such middle leader skills and experiences. Deborah is flattered to be asked to do this.

Though Deborah may be flattered to be considered to take on this role she needs to enquire from the head teacher what training and support will she be offered to do this role effectively. Before Deborah says yes she may like to visit other colleagues in her setting or another setting to allow her to talk with and ask questions of an established mentor. She may like to ask, if she takes on this task, whether she will be given time to do this role effectively. This may involve visiting the school's partner training institution. Mentor training will allow Deborah to meet other mentors and the school's partner institute's staff and to understand the roles and responsibilities that may go with the job. It will also help Deborah to consider what knowledge, skills and attitudes are needed to be successful in this position as well as allowing her to establish a network of other colleagues to support her in this role.

School-based mentors like Deborah can learn how to carry out the role through support, advice and training offered by ITT institutions. Such support would seem invaluable given, as the Teaching Schools Council (2016, p.11) suggests:

ITT providers that have invested in effective mentoring will support trainees to become high-quality teachers, and build their resilience so that they are more likely to remain in teaching once their initial training is complete.

It is important to note, however, that the Teaching Schools Council (2016, p.11) indicates that head teachers as well as ITT providers have a vital role to play in the identification, training, monitoring and continuing support for mentors.

Critics of school-based mentoring and the lack of its successful nurturing in schools, including Hobson and Malderez (2013), have, however, blamed some of its shortcomings on national policy, which has not given mentoring sufficient status. This may also be seen alongside the need for more appropriate/rigorous selection and training of mentors. Most importantly and fundamentally, however:

policy-makers might be said to have failed to promote effectively a common understanding of what mentoring ought to entail or what mentors should be seeking to achieve. (Hobson and Malderez, 2013, p.10)

Mentoring courses do, however, exist through institutions such as universities, in order to support and equip those undertaking a mentoring role. These seek to provide the tools and techniques mentors require to support, grow and develop. However, what appears to be lacking, as identified by the Carter Review of initial teacher training (Carter, 2015), is the coherent and consistent school-based mentoring of trainee teachers. This should be seen alongside the need for a greater status and recognition of this role in a trainee's development. For Carter (2015, p.12), effective mentoring has many benefits, including: 'providing professional development opportunities for mentors and building the capacity of the school as a whole'. For Carter (2015), effective mentors should be outstanding teachers and subject experts, as well as accomplished individuals who are skilled in explaining their own practice.

From this review of the state of mentoring, as it related to initial teacher training, was borne a recognition of the need for a set of national standards. Although non-statutory, they represent – at present – the best attempt to address the many issues and concerns raised by Carter (2015) and seek to promote an enhanced coherence and consistency of mentoring for trainee teachers.

KEY REFLECTIONS

- How you did you become a mentor?
- What do you see as the benefits and drawbacks of being a school-based mentor?

THE MENTOR STANDARDS

In response to the recommendations outlined by the Carter Review (2015), the Teaching Schools Council (aided by head teachers and ITT leads from teaching schools with experience of working in school-based ITT settings) were commissioned by the government with: 'helping to promote the importance of the [mentor] role and creat[ing] a better shared understanding of the characteristics of effective mentoring across the ITT sector' (Teaching Schools Council, 2016, p.5).

The Teaching Schools Council (2016) produced a set of non-statutory national standards for school-based ITT mentors known as the Mentor Standards. The accompanying guidance clearly suggests that the role of mentoring should extend to those in the early stages of their teaching career. For researchers such as Shields and Murray (2017, p.328) such standards are seen to:

reflect many of the needs of beginning teachers in terms of 'belonging' and 'pedagogical support', and it will be interesting to see to what extent they impact beginning teachers' experiences during school placements.

These Mentor Standards were allied to the Teachers' Standards (DfE, 2011) and were underpinned by a recognition of the central role that mentors play in supporting trainee teachers. This support is seen to be strengthened by excellent subject knowledge, a clear view of what constitutes high-quality teaching and a wealth of experience regarding the strategies and techniques that could be best used to support trainees.

Though the Teaching Schools Council (2016, p.7) acknowledge the role that an ITT course structure and content could play in a trainee teacher's training, they also suggest that careful thought is needed about the best way to train and value mentors not only when teachers become mentors but also in terms of their ongoing support. This would enable:

mentors to further improve their practice by training them in how to deconstruct and articulate their practice, how to coach and how to support and assess trainee teachers effectively.

For other contributors to this review, such as Tom Bennett and his expert group, behaviour management was seen as a vital part of training for trainee teachers, with this being delivered by those: 'with impeccable skills and understanding in this area' (Teaching Schools Council, 2016, p.7). This recommendation is underpinned, where necessary, by the need for ITT providers not only to locate and train mentors/tutors and coaches with accomplished abilities, but also those skilled in promoting successful behaviour practices with regard to teaching.

For the Teaching Schools Council (2016), mentoring should be seen in terms of a valued partnership between ITT providers and school-based colleagues, with schools establishing a positive climate which enables trainee teachers to achieve professional expectations. As outlined by the Teaching Schools Council (2016), such a partnership may go some way to address the concerns of researchers – including Hobson and Malderez (2013) – who have suggested that mentors are unfamiliar with a student's university-based course requirements and content. It is also important that schools should provide time for mentors to monitor progress, observe, feedback and have meetings outside of class-based time.

For the Teaching Schools Council (2016), succession planning was also of vital importance, not only to provide high-quality mentor support for trainees, but also to support the retention and availability of mentoring and high-quality partnership placements.

Though these suggestions have great value, it is important that the mentors should take some responsibility in this vital school/ITT partnership. Whilst recommendations can be made about ways in which mentoring can be enhanced it is important to recognise a teacher's own professional role in supporting high-quality mentoring. As the Teaching Schools Council (2016, p.8) noted, this includes mentor's having:

- an understanding of course structure

- knowledge of the requirement or trainees to meet the Teachers' Standards

- a wish to prioritise meetings and discussions with a trainee

- a desire to monitor performance so as to develop their teaching practice

- a need to promote effective classroom management strategies

- up-to-date subject knowledge as well as an ability to signpost trainees to other forms of expertise and knowledge – for example, subject associations.

USING THE MENTOR STANDARDS

As authors with first-hand knowledge and experiences of school-based mentoring and its links to ITT, we can recognise much of what has been discussed throughout this chapter. As with both the Carter Review (2015) and the General Teaching Council (2016), we similarly see a need for high-quality mentoring and strong ITT/school mentoring partnerships so as to consistently promote high-quality practice and the development of outstanding trainee and early career teachers. We, alongside the Teaching Schools Council (2016), seek to raise the profile of mentoring, and of mentors, within schools. We also hope that this book will provide a means to strengthen mentors' subject knowledge, facilitate an understanding of what high-quality mentoring skills might look like and suggest some strategies and techniques that mentors would like to use when supporting their mentees.

This book has been designed to support school-based mentors whether they are new to the role or are more established mentors. It is based around the outlined foci and non-statutory standards laid out by the Teaching Schools Council (2016, p.11). The initial chapters are:

- Chapter 2 – Standard 1: Personal qualities

- Chapter 3 – Standard 2: Teaching

- Chapter 4 – Standard 3: Professionalism

- Chapter 5 – Standard 4: Self-development and working in partnership.

For current mentors, each chapter will allow you an opportunity to reflect upon your own practice as a mentor in relation to trainee and early career teachers. It will allow you, as an individual, to consider a better understanding of the extent of your current role and to identify your strengths and areas for development. This book may prove useful for those of you who manage mentors, given that each chapter may act as a self-audit tool and/or a basis on which future mentor training could be based.

Finally, this book has also been written as a useful reference text for people who may wish to become mentors. As such it refers to research which underpins the notion of mentoring. This book will enable ITT institution/school partnership staff to reflect on how they train and support their school-based mentor partners, and also to consider whether their mentors currently exhibit the skills and qualities needed to be effective and whether additional professional development/ professional courses would be appropriate for them so that they more effectively undertake such duties.

The final chapters are:

- Chapter 6 – Professional mentoring skills

- Chapter 7 – Models and techniques for mentoring.

Both chapters build upon topics outlined in Chapters 2–5 and enable mentors to reflect upon their practice and build upon their existing knowledge and skills. Chapter 6 outlines some key mentoring skills, along with tips that a mentor may find useful, and Chapter 7 discusses some models and techniques drawn from theoretical perspectives, such as solution-focused coaching, cognitive behavioural coaching and motivational interviewing, that mentors can put into practice. As with the earlier chapters, it is our intention that the content can form the basis for a self-audit in relation to the theory and practice linked to current mentoring and seeks to aid development as an effective school mentor.

KEY REFLECTIONS

- How might you define your current mentoring role?

- What are the benefits and drawbacks of being a mentor?

- What key knowledge, skills and attitudes do you have to be an outstanding school mentor?

- What strategies are currently in place to support your role and professional development?

- How can schools and ITT partnerships work together to support the development of your mentoring role in school?

CHAPTER SUMMARY

- There are various routes that trainee teachers may take to obtain QTS and become outstanding teachers as outlined by the Teachers' Standards (2011).

- A partnership is needed between ITT providers and schools to promote effective mentoring.

- The role of school-based mentoring has grown over successive years.

- Mentoring can play a significant part in supporting trainee teachers and early career teachers.

- Mentees need support in developing the knowledge, skills and attitudes needed to become an outstanding professional.

- Mentoring can promote emotional resilience against the stresses experienced by fledgling teachers.

(Continued)

(Continued)

- The National Mentor Standards (Teaching Schools Council, 2016) outline a mentor's role and guide the support required by trainee teachers and early career teachers.

- There are various means by which teachers become school-based mentors and it is therefore important to provide them with professional development to ensure they are able to fulfil their duties.

SELF-AUDIT QUESTIONS

- How would you define mentoring?

- Why is a successful partnership needed to support mentoring in schools?

- Why is effective mentoring important for trainee teachers and early career teachers?

- What are the skills, attitudes and areas of knowledge needed by outstanding school mentors?

- Why is there a need for a set of National Mentor Standards?

SUGGESTED ADDITIONAL READING

Aderibigbe, S., Gray, D.S. and Colucci-Gray, L. (2018) Understanding the nature of mentoring experiences between teachers and student teachers. *International Journal of Mentoring and Coaching in Education*, 7(1), 54–71.

Department for Education (2019) *Early Career Framework*. Available at https://assets.publishing.service.gov.uk/government/uploads/system/uploads/attachment_data/file/773705/Early-Career_Framework.pdf (accessed 4 April 2019).

Marable, M.A. and Raimondi, S.L. (2007) Teachers' perceptions of what was most (and least) supportive during their first year of teaching. *Mentoring and Tutoring*, 15(1), 25–37.

Peiser, G., Ambrose, J. Burke, B. and Davenport, J. (2018) The role of the mentor in professional knowledge development across four professions. *International Journal of Mentoring and Coaching in Education*, 7(1), 2–18.

Spooner-Lane, R. (2017) Mentor and beginning teachers in primary schools: research review. *Professional Development in Education*, 43(2), 253–73.

REFERENCES

Aspfors, J. and Fransson, G. (2015) Research on mentor education for mentors of newly qualified teachers: a qualitative meta-synthesis. *Teaching and Teacher Education*, 48, 75–86.

ATL Media Office (2017) *New Teachers Already Demotivated about Teaching at the Start of their Careers*. Available at https://www.atl.org.uk/latest/new-teachers-already-demotivated-about-teaching-start-their-careers (accessed 11 January 2019).

Bressman, S., Winter, J.S. and Efat Efron, S. (2018) Next generation mentoring: supporting teachers beyond induction. *Teaching and Teacher Education*, 73, 162–70.

Bullough, R.V. and Hall-Kenyon, K.M. (2012) On teacher hope, sense of calling, and commitment to teaching. *Teacher Education Quarterly*, Spring.

Carter, A. (2015) Carter Review of Initial Teacher Training. Available at https://www.gov.uk/government/publications/carter-review-of-initial-teacher-training (accessed 26 February 2019).

CUREE (2005) *Mentoring and Coaching CPD Capacity Building Project: National Framework for Mentoring and Coaching*. Available at http://www.curee.co.uk/files/publication/1219925968/National-framework-for-mentoring-and-coaching.pdf (accessed 3 February 2019).

Day, C., Sammons, P., Stobart, G., Kington, A. and Gu, Q. (2007) *Teachers Matter: Connecting Work, Lives, and Effectiveness*. Maidenhead: Open University Press.

Department for Education (DfE) (2011) Teachers' Standards: Guidance for School Leaders, School Staff and Governing Bodies. Available at: https://assets.publishing.service.gov.uk/government/uploads/system/uploads/attachment_data/file/665520/Teachers__Standards.pdf (accessed 9 November 2018).

Department for Education (2018a), *Early career CPD: exploratory research: research report, November 2018*. Available at: https://www.gov.uk/government/publications/early-career-continuing-professional-development-cpd-research (accessed 3rd February 2019).

Department for Education (2018b) *Induction for Newly Qualified Teachers (England)*. Available at https://assets.publishing.service.gov.uk/government/uploads/system/uploads/attachment_data/file/696428/Statutory_Induction_Guidance_2018.pdf (accessed 4 April 2019).

Department for Education (2019) *Early Career Framework*. Available at https://assets.publishing.service.gov.uk/government/uploads/system/uploads/attachment_data/file/773705/Early-Career_Framework.pdf (accessed 4 April 2019).

Flores, M.A. and Day, C. (2006) Contexts which shape and reshape new teachers' identities: a multi-perspective study. *Teaching and Teacher Education*, 22(2), 219–32.

Gardiner, W. and Weisling, N. (2018) Challenges and complexities of developing mentors' practice: insights from new mentors. *International Journal of Mentoring and Coaching in Education*, 7(4), 329-432.

Gove, M. (2010) Speech, Michael Gove to the National College Annual Conference, Birmingham. Available at https://www.gov.uk/government/speeches/michael-gove-to-the-national-college-annual-conference-birmingham (accessed 3 January 2019).

Hobson, A.J. and Malderez, A. (2013) Judgementoring and other threats to realizing the potential of school-based mentoring in teacher education. *International Journal of Mentoring and Coaching in Education*, 2(2), 89–108.

Hobson, A.J., Ashby, P., Maderez, A. and Tomlinson, P. (2009) Mentoring beginning teachers: what we know and what we don't. *Teaching and Teacher Education*, 25, 207–16.

Huberman, M. (1993) *The Lives of Teachers*. London and New York: Cassell and Teachers College Press.

Izadinia, M. (2016) Student teachers' and mentor-teachers' perceptions and expectations of a mentoring relationship: do they match or class. *Professional Development in Education*, 42(3), 387–402.

Lindgren, U. (2007) Experiences of beginning teachers in a school-based mentoring program in Sweden. *Educational Studies*, 31(3), 251–63.

Marable, M.A. and Raimondi, S.L. (2007) Teachers' perceptions of what was most (and least) supportive during their first year of teaching. *Mentoring and Tutoring*, 15(1), 25–37.

National Audit Office (2016) *Training New Teachers*. Available at https://www.nao.org.uk/wp-content/uploads/2016/02/Training-new-teachers.pdf (accessed 12 April 2019).

Passmore, J., Brown, H., Csigas, Z. et al. (2017) *The State of Play in European Coaching and Mentoring: Executive Report 2017*. Available at: https://assets.henley.ac.uk/defaultUploads/The-State-of-Play-in-European-Coaching-Mentoring-Executive-Report-2017.pdf?mtime=20 (accessed 3 February 2019).

Roberts, A. (2000) Mentoring revisited: a phenomenological reading of the literature. *Mentoring and Tutoring*, 8(2), 145–70.

Roehrig, A.D., Bohn, C.M., Turner, J.E. and Pressley, M. (2008) Mentoring beginning teachers for exemplary practices. *Teaching and Teacher Education*, 24, 684–702.

Shields, S. and Murray, M. (2017) Beginning teachers' perceptions of mentors and access to communities of practice. *International Journal of Mentoring and Coaching in Education*, 6(4), 317–31.

Teaching Schools Council (2016) *National Standards for School-Based Initial Teacher Training (ITT) Mentors*. Available at https://assets.publishing.service.gov.uk/government/uploads/system/uploads/attachment_data/file/536891/Mentor_standards_report_Final.pdf (accessed 2 January 2019).

2

STANDARD 1: PERSONAL QUALITIES

CHAPTER OBJECTIVES

By the end of this chapter you should be aware of:

- the role that trust, empathy, modelling of professional practice and relationships play in effective mentoring
- the role that personal values play in a mentoring
- the need for clear boundaries and expectations to define and enhance relationships when mentoring
- that modelling of professional practice by a mentor and their colleagues allows mentees to critically reflect upon and improve their own professional practice
- that empathy forms part of a dynamic relationship between mentor and mentee, helping them to appreciate the feelings of each individual.

MENTOR STANDARDS

This chapter supports the development of the following Mentor Standards (Teaching Schools Council, 2016, p.10):

- Trusting relationships
- Modelling high standards of practice
- Empathising with the challenges a trainee faces.

INTRODUCTION

This chapter focuses on several important factors with regard to being an effective mentor. It includes the significant part that *trust* can play in a mentor/mentee relationship, the ability a mentor has to show *empathy* with mentees and the role that the *modelling* of professional practice can have in promoting outstanding trainees and early career teachers. This chapter will allow mentors an opportunity to reflect on their own knowledge, understanding and current experiences, in particular linked to the factors outlined above. It will consider the current knowledge base, research and practices relating to trust, empathy and modelling. Importantly, it will give mentors an opportunity to benchmark themselves against multiple perspectives regarding these items. It will provide mentors, through reflection, with an opportunity to question not only their 'understanding' but also their 'attitudes and their actions' (Nahmad-Williams, 2013, p.178) in relation to such important factors.

PERSONAL AND PROFESSIONAL MENTORING

Before considering the factors of trust, empathy and modelling of professional practice, it should be acknowledged that for trainees and early career teachers the 'playing field' on which mentoring is based can be far from level. Factors such as the time a mentor has been in post and the context in which the mentee is placed will play an important role in the quality of mentoring which may be delivered. Researchers such as Hudson (2007), for example, would suggest that as well as a wide range of mentoring expertise across settings this may also extend to subject-level expertise.

PERSONAL VALUES

Allied to the factors outlined above, it is vital that both mentor and mentee acknowledge the role that personal values can play in the process of mentoring. Such personal and professional dispositions will have an impact upon how you, as a mentor, carry out your role. How can you have an empathic relationship with a mentee regarding the challenges they may face, build up trust with them or model high standards of practice towards them unless you know what values and beliefs you hold dear. With such knowledge, you may be better able to be mindful of your responses to mentees which result from your own views and opinions to certain situations. Similarly, each mentee's views and reactions to an individual scenario, as with yours, will reflect their own personally held views and beliefs. As Woolley (2013) suggests, a teaching professional's core values will influence perceived goals when educating. Therefore, when you engage in reflection around this chapter, start to consider:

- how well you know your mentee

- how well you know yourself

- whether you have found time to talk to your mentee about their, and your own, personal and professional values and beliefs

- whether you know where your mentee is coming from when they are professionally challenged, or when they are finding constructive criticism difficult.

PERSONAL INVESTMENT

Remember everyone's view of self is different and this, in turn, will impact upon their own developing professional identity – that is, professional identity is seen in terms of how they define themselves and others (Day et al., 2007). Mentoring goes well beyond just inculcating professional knowledge and the giving of practical self; it inevitably involves an investment of yourself and this, no doubt, will have many benefits and drawbacks. However, by providing such a welcoming commitment to those new to the profession you can support your mentee, who may feel, in the beginning, they do not belong; who may feel they are on the periphery; and may not feel like a 'real teacher' (Shields and Murray, 2017, p.325).

The role of mentoring will inevitably lead you to use a significant amount of your emotional intelligence. Mentoring will involve trust, care and intimacy, as well as being seen to be part of a continuum which allows for autonomy and difference in a mentor/mentee relationship (Chun et al., 2010). It will no doubt be a pleasure when things are going well in your mentoring relationships; however, it can be more challenging when things are not going as planned. Given the personal investment in supporting a mentee, if tensions and issues arise it may become hard to stay objective and to avoid emotive responses. Therefore, it is vital that you are prepared for such a scenario, given the need to sustain a positive working relationship. For researchers such as Hudson and Hudson (2018), how you resolve tensions will depend on the intensity of the issue as well as how committed individuals are to reaching a resolution. Consider therefore, before you undertake mentoring, whether you have a clear:

- understanding of the issues that can cause tension

- set of expectations about the relationship you will be entering into

- indication of the conduct that each of you can expect in the relationship

- procedure to share your concerns with a third party if a relationship breaks down, so as to provide for mediation. (Hudson and Hudson, 2018)

A clear code of conduct (jointly agreed with your mentee) can go a long way to building up a positive mentoring relationship on which professional relationships may grow.

KEY REFLECTIONS

- How does trust, empathy and modelling currently fit into your mentoring practice?

- How important do you consider these factors in promoting outstanding trainee and early career practice?

MENTORING RELATIONSHIPS

As a mentor, a relationship with your trainee and early career teacher will be pivotal in developing positive outcomes for them. As the Mentor Standards indicate (Teaching Schools Council, 2016, p.11), it will involve you being able to 'make time for the trainee' as well as 'prioritising meeting and discussion'. In a busy school this will often prove difficult given the demands of your job and the role of being a mentor. To help solve such an issue, and to help secure quality time for supporting your mentee, you may find the use of shared planning, preparation and assessment time (PPA) beneficial. Such a decision, however, must ultimately be left to individuals to decide what works best for them. Whatever you decide, it is important you set clear expectations and have a focused agenda to work to in such meetings. This will allow you to prioritise the important issues and for associated paperwork to be completed.

The need to 'be approachable' (Teaching Schools Council, 2016, p.11) will form the basis of your working relationships with your mentee. It will be underpinned by a need to approach your role using effective interpersonal skills so that you are best placed to support your mentee whether professionally or personally (e.g. how they are feeling regarding their progress and attainment) with regard to the Teachers' Standards (DfE, 2011). Many of these interpersonal skills will be covered in later chapters of this book (such as Chapter 6: Professional mentoring skills).

However, this chapter will now turn its attention to the need for trust and empathy between you and your mentee, as well as the role that you and your colleagues can play in modelling high standards of practice (the topic of planning, teaching and assessment will be covered in more detail in Chapter 3: Teaching) to support their effective and outstanding practice.

MENTORING AND TRUST

PERSONAL RELATIONSHIPS

As Kyriacou et al. (2003) and Thornton (1999) suggest, the relationship between a mentee and a mentor must be seen as the key to success or failure when undertaking teacher training. Such a relationship may be considered as social and dynamic in its nature and it will involve the 'use of emotional information in reasoning and behaviour' – i.e. that of emotional intelligence (Chun et al., 2010, p.422) – so that trust may be built. As Chun et al. (2010) indicate, positive emotions will underpin and promote the foundations of the development of trust. Part of such ties will involve care and a real interest in the mentee. However, given this, there will be a real need for a professional distance to be kept in any mentoring relationship so as to avoid the dangers and situations that may occur given too close an emotional tie. Though you may, at times, utter very wise words of advice to a mentee it will be the emotionally wise responses which most matter.

TRUST IN A RELATIONSHIP

A trusting relationship is pivotal to effective mentoring, alongside respect, and freedom of expression between one another (Gehrke and Kay, 1984; Thomas and Smith, 2009; Hobson et al., 2009; Chun et al., 2010; Jones et al., 2019). Trust will be important when and if things are not going well for your mentee. It is important that they feel that they do not have to suffer in silence, that they can open up and be honest so as to avoid any such feeling having a negative impact upon their mental health and well-being (Howard et al., 2019). It is not, however, a foregone conclusion that trust will be immediate and necessarily enduring between you and your mentee. For such a relationship to develop, and be successful, there needs to be a willingness on the part of mentee to be mentored (Hobson et al., 2009). Such a willingness may be linked to the specific context: whether the mentor is deemed suitable, has the necessary characteristics to be effective and is well prepared and able to employ relevant strategies to mentoring (Hobson et al., 2009).

'Trusting relationships' form part of Mentor Standard 1 and are vital to your future relationships with individuals (Teaching Schools Council, 2016, p.10). Therefore, it is important for you to consider, as a mentor, that beginner teachers wish to be wanted, accepted and welcomed in the classroom (Shield and Murray, 2017). You, no doubt, will do this without knowing it, but do consider what verbal and non-verbal messages you give out when you first meet your mentee. How do you:

- show your interest in having them in your class?

- remain predictable in the way in which you deal with situations that involve the mentee?

- remain fair and consistent in your approach to your mentee?

- maintain your active listening?

- indicate that that the mentee has a clear say in the mentoring relationship?

As your mentoring relationships develop, it is important that you develop and sustain effective communication and social interaction skills (Hudson and Hudson, 2018) which Hudson outlines as being 'attentive listening, high level listening skills, and having a sense of humour' (2013, p.115). Trust will be vital if there is to be a comfortable co-relationship when talking to your mentee about teaching and when reflecting on the process of their practice (Hudson, 2005). As a mentor, through your relationship with the mentee, you can 'identify and interrogate critically their (the mentee's) conceptions of teaching, of learning to teach and of mentoring' (Hobson et al., 2009, p.212).

CHALLENGES TO TRUST

However, any trusting approach you develop will be underpinned by the challenge of combining support with accountability and assessment (O'Sullivan and Conway, 2016). More than ever, at such a point, the need for 'open dialogue' will be key alongside a 'non-threatening reciprocal relationship' borne out of respect for the ideas and experiences that can be brought to your relationship with the mentee (Jones et al., 2019). Such a need to assess and be accountable in practice will sometimes be allied to negative issues which centre on the notion of judgemental mentoring ... described as 'judgementoring' by Hobson and Malderez (2013, p.89). With you, as a mentor, acting as an assessor and gatekeeper to the profession, judgementoring is a requirement for you (Hobson and Malderez, 2013, p.101). What may be seen as 'powerful networks' between individuals, are often centred on personal similarities and high levels of trust and of shared values (Dhillon, 2009, p.701). For an individual to feel safe, for them to feel they are able to ask for support and for scaffolding of their learning to take place trust will be vital (Stanulis and Russell, 2000). The building of trust may be considered, by some, as a form of 'social capital' that underpins successful partnership working and relationships

(Dhillon, 2009, p.687). As Dhillon (2009, p.701) notes, trust – allied to shared norms and values – will allow for the formation of what may be termed as a 'social glue' (Dhillon, 2009, p.701).

KEY REFLECTIONS

- How aware are you of your emotions when working with your mentees?
- How do you promote the role of being a critical friend?
- How do you think being a trainee/early career teacher's assessor impacts upon your relationship with them?

MODELLING HIGH STANDARDS OF PRACTICE

As mentors you will all be different – for example, in terms of your own beliefs and your view of what is important in order to promote outstanding teaching and learning and how best to organise and manage class-based procedures. Differences may also occur in the way you teach, plan and assess as a mentor. As Hobson et al. suggest, you will play an important part in helping your mentee adapt to the 'norms, standards and expectations associated with teaching in general and with specific schools' (2009, p.209).

Each school context will be different. Mentoring will therefore play a crucial role in seeing how individuals' professional practice can vary. This may be in terms of how each individual may be seen – that is, as an organiser and/or a challenger of learning (Wang and Odell, 2002). For researchers such as Shields and Murray (2017, p.326), pedagogical support for those who are 'beginner teachers' will centre on regular guidance and advice linked to assessment, planning and class-based practices. One key feature of support will no doubt involve you acting as an adviser and information source (Shields and Murray, 2017).

MODELLING PRACTICE

Modelling how you plan teaching and learning will enable your mentees to see how you approach time management, classroom organisation, curricular content, progression and the means by which assessment will be undertaken to inform future learning progression – all useful exposure to professional practice. It will be important that you, as a mentor, also point out that differences in such professional practices – due to, for example, the school's leadership, ethos and demographics – will inevitably occur. This will make it hard for you, at times, to give definitive statements of practice to a mentee, given such variations in factors. For some researchers, issues may also centre on mentors being sufficiently skilled to mentor a large range of primary subjects (Hudson, 2007). All of these items will no doubt prove challenging in the context of promoting the knowledge, skills and understanding of trainee and early career teachers around how to be an outstanding teacher of the future.

The need for the development of an individual's practice has clear resonance with the Mentor Standards, which also value improving a 'trainee's teaching by modelling exemplary practice in planning, teaching and assessment' (Teaching Schools Council, 2016, p.11). As a mentor, the one key strategy in your armoury to support and develop an individual's practice may be found through the use of a trainee/early career teacher's observations and discussion around modelled lessons. For researchers such as Jones et al. (2019) learning conversations based on an individual's tangible teaching experience allows the mentee with an opportunity not only to be supported but also encouraged. Such modelling of practice, subject knowledge and progression of learning may be invaluable, especially with regard to subject specific teaching. For example, researchers such as Blackmore, Howard and Kington, (2018, p.14) clearly showed that postgraduate trainee teachers' school-based opportunities to observe and teach science had a direct impact on shaping their professional identities as well as their confidence in teaching primary science. As trainees they 'aspired to see context-specific modelling of science teaching in order to effectively reflect upon their own levels of efficacy' (Blackmore, Howard and Kington, 2018, p.14). Any class-based observations of practice will usually be followed by an associated review meeting to discuss the findings. As suggested by Jones et al. (2018, p.135), mentor feedback may be seen over time to move from a more 'standardised formal feedback' – which wishes to build confidence as well as 'general and basic pedagogical practices' – to a more dialogic approach, with feedback being more critical and personalised in order to challenge a mentee's approach to teaching and learning (Jones et al., 2018). It is important to acknowledge such feedback will often not only be confined to a singular conversation or time; feedback will continually happen outside both the time and space of a review meeting. As Jones et al. (2019, p.129) suggest, successful mentoring is an 'immersive process' where the mentee and mentor are repeatedly challenged not only in terms of teaching and learning, but also by the need to establish and develop 'a relationship that is conducive to shared learning'.

As with Sonia's case study below, mentees can learn a lot through skilled observation and questioning of your own, and others', professional practice. For academics such as Certo (2005), a mentor's relationship with their mentee can lead to a mentee's reflection on their practice and facilitation of the sharing of ideas between mentor and mentee. For other researchers, such as Hudson (2013, p.116), observations are seen by mentors as being necessary in order for individuals to start to understand pedagogical decisions and classroom contexts.

For mentees to get the most out of such opportunities, you should consider:

- agreeing objectives and identifying a clear focus for an observation

- entering into a genuine dialogue, where you are happy to have the strengths/ weakness of your practice explored

- giving consideration to the reasoning for such a professional approach

- giving clear actions so that developmental ideas come out of this practice for the mentee

- an agreed timescale for a future focused observation for observing the impact and implementation of learned developmental points.

For such an opportunity for learning to be successful, you must agree clear ground rules and be prepared for some likely praise and potential questioning of your own practice. Such learning can prove the real test of an open and frank relationship.

CASE STUDY: SONIA

When reflecting upon her experiences of teaching, following a class-based observation as part of her second placement, Sonia's mentor Alison commented on the pace of Sonia's lesson and the need for her to reflect upon how she could more effectively model concepts and deal with misconceptions in her lesson. Sonia is unsure what this may look like in practice and is wondering how she might develop these aspects of her practice.

To support Sonia, Alison could suggest that they co-plan the next lesson together so that they can both identify aspects of learning that may be problematic or may be part of a common misconception. Alison could then teach the lesson, with Sonia observing how Alison develops the pace in her lesson and the strategies she uses to model and scaffold learning. Alison could then suggest that Sonia puts timings onto her lesson plan to make her reflect on

(Continued)

(Continued)

the pace of her teaching and learning. She could also encourage Sonia to visit other teachers with the focus being on how they model learning and how they promote pace in their lessons. These actions could then be reviewed and discussed after they have happened so as to reflect on what Sonia has learned and the future actions needed to develop her teaching and learning. It is important that trainee and early career teachers are allowed to experience and observe a range of professional practice within your setting. As with Sonia, this can be achieved by enabling mentees to see a range of successful teachers operate within your setting.

For those mentoring trainees and early career teachers in small school settings, an observation of others' professional practice may sometimes prove problematic as the result of the small number of experienced teachers available for mentees to visit and learn from. Such limitations may also be compounded when one such experienced teacher is, in fact, the school's teaching head teacher. With such a scenario potentially inhibiting trainee or early career teachers from revealing issues and concerns they may be experiencing with their practice given this person's high status, it may be necessary for you to seek further observational opportunities in another mentor colleague's setting.

EXPERIENCING A RANGE OF PRACTICE

As Hudson (2013) indicates, positive teaching experiences will not only aid mentees to grow professionally but can also lead to improved teacher self-efficacy. Such practical class-based experiences may go some way to negate the criticism of researchers such as Wang and Odell (2002) regarding trainees' involvement in institutional coursework. By allowing school mentees to experience a range of teaching, it may serve to provide a means to challenge and change trainees' existing beliefs and practices (Wang and Odell, 2002).

Enabling mentees to engage with a range of teaching and teachers has clear links with the views of Wenger (2000) who suggests that being new to a community will involve experiencing their world as part of a social learning environment. This will enable ways of belonging, engagement (i.e. the co-construction of meaning) and imagination (developing an image of themselves), as well as alignment (striving to achieve a goal by interpreting actions) all of which can help each individual align themselves to their community of practice (Wenger, 2000, p.421). However, it is important to acknowledge that being new to any organisation or community of practice is not easy – researchers such as Lave and Wenger (1991, p.29), for example, suggest such 'legitimate peripheral participation' involves an inequality of power in the relationship. However, despite such a point, surely one clear benefit of a relationship between a mentor and mentee must be that of, at times, acting as a critical friend. This will involve being a person who asks provocative questions and provides a critique of a mentee's practice (Kutsyuruba and Walker, 2015, p.33). This is necessary to avoid a criticism made of mentors, by researchers such as Hudson, who suggest that 'there is little evidence that mentors encourage mentees to think critically about their practices' (2007, p.204).

For many trainees and early career teachers, such exposure to a range of teaching practices will give them an opportunity to reflect upon their own practice, as well allowing them to experience the multiple perspectives around models of professional expertise and practice. Such sharing of experiences, and exposure to a range of practice, may in turn help shape a trainee's and early career teacher's professional identity (Hong, 2010; Beijaard et al., 2004).

Such exposure to a range of professional practice beyond your own, may go some way to help avoid a criticism levelled at mentoring by researchers such as Wang and Odell (2002), who indicate that mentors' roles in relation to early career teachers relate more to logistical and technical support than supporting them regarding, for example, curriculum matters.

Allowing mentees to see others in your school modelling a range of teaching practices may have a positive effect way beyond that of the mentor and mentee relationship. In terms of the wider school, it requires managers and mentors to know their staff, their strengths and areas of expertise. For those staff involved, it may also allow them to experience a mentor's world which, in turn, may not only be good professional development but may lead to others considering such a role as part of their career progression.

EMPATHY AND MENTORING

Whatever the situation you find yourself in with mentoring, you will need to have a clear expectation of a mentoring/mentee relationship. This will include being non-judgemental, approachable, a good listener and having the ability to show empathy (Hobson et al., 2009). For other researchers, such as Jordan and Schwartz, such interactions and relationships with students may help individuals to understand others in order to 'balance support, and standards, role boundaries, and the power of connection in teaching and learning' (2018, p.1).

Empathy will form part of a dynamic relationship and will involve you becoming emotionally self-aware so as to fully appreciate the feeling of others. For authors such as Pask and Joy (2007) 'empathy' is a term which may get confused with the notion of sympathy. As Pask and Joy suggest, sympathy should be considered to be 'feeling with' whereas empathy is a 'feeling into' an individual's situation and feelings (Pask and Joy, 2007, p.122). It involves a process linked to a state of mind: a mental and emotional struggle which may be linked to one of the competencies within Goleman's (1998) Emotional Intelligence framework. Jordan and Schwartz (2018) suggest that the feeling of empathy goes well beyond an acknowledgement of another's feelings, noting that, for empathy to have a real impact and to bring about change, it must form a mutual feeling, of another being touched. As with Sunil's case study below, John is able to have real empathy with Sunil's situation given his experiences of teaching. Such a connection will generate a real feeling of support for Sunil. At times, empathy will enable you to feel positively towards a mentee and the situation they find themselves in; at other times, you may experience frustration towards them.

For authors such as Pask and Joy the essence of empathy will rest upon active, empathic listening. As they note 'the way in which we listen and communicate can develop a clear sense of empathy of which both participants are aware' (2007, p.124). It is important to note, however, that finding out what a mentee is really feeling may be difficult at times, given the power dynamic of the mentor/mentee relationship. It may also be difficult for you to truly empathise with your mentee if they are reluctant, for example, to open up regarding their performance or abilities regarding poor levels of behaviour management.

CASE STUDY: SUNIL

Sunil is on his first placement and is finding it hard to deal with one particular pupil who has quite disruptive behaviour. Sunil is trying to be friendly, but is lacking in authority when dealing with this situation. It is shaking his confidence and the feelings that he wishes to be a teacher in the future. He has started to open up about these feelings in his weekly review with his mentor, John.

John is really glad that Sunil trusts him enough to talk to him about his issues and feelings around teaching. It is a big thing to do this, given John's position of power as Sunil's mentor. It is important that John spends as much time as he can with Sunil at this meeting so that what he says is given value. John must be aware of the non-verbal messages he gives when he actively listens to his mentee. John can show empathy with Sunil by suggesting Sunil's feelings are normal for most teachers as they doubt their abilities when they start teaching; they can struggle with difficult children and this can shake confidence in their own abilities. John must make certain he keeps reassuring Sunil and emphasises that he can come to see John to talk and that this will be non-judgemental. John must be clear on the action points needed to support Sunil, including strategies to help him with the child who is shaking his confidence.

As Barr (2011) notes, at times empathy will not always be enough to improve and resolve a situation. Though you may have an ability to empathise with a situation, as a mentor you will be aware of the major ramifications of certain issues, such as a trainee's lack of behaviour management, upon the class. Given such a situation, at times there will be a desire to balance the needs of your mentee against the need for decisive action to avoid an ongoing situation which is detrimental to the well-being of others.

KEY REFLECTIONS

- How might your personal values influence your role as a mentor?
- What do you consider to be the key skills you need to be an effective mentor?
- How might you establish a trusting relationship between you and your mentee?
- Why is modelling of outstanding practice vital for a mentee's professional development?
- Why is empathy a key factor in being an effective mentor?

CHAPTER SUMMARY

- Personal values, emotional intelligence and a conducive mentoring environment can influence the process and relational aspects of mentoring.

(Continued)

(Continued)

- Trust, respect and freedom of expression should be seen as pivotal to effective mentoring when acting as a critical friend.

- Trust may be difficult given the mentor role includes assessing a mentee's teaching ability.

- Modelling of professional practice and personal reflection can develop a mentee's understanding of pedagogical practice and decision-making.

- Empathy will allow for an appreciation of the feeling of others and will involve active and empathic listening by the mentor.

SELF-AUDIT QUESTIONS

- What do you understand by the term 'empathy', and how might you have shown this in your mentoring?

- What do you understand by the term 'trust', and how might you have shown this in your mentoring?

- What do you understand by the term 'modelling of practice', and how might you have shown this in your mentoring?

- What are the skills and attitudes needed to promote empathy and trust between mentor and mentee?

- Why are trust, empathy and modelling vital to securing outstanding trainee/early career practice?

SUGGESTED ADDITIONAL READING

Blackmore, K., Howard, C. and Kington, A. (2018) Trainee teachers' experience of primary science teaching, and the perceived impact on their developing professional identity. *European Journal of Teacher Education*, 1–20. ISSN 0261-9768 Online.

Day, C., Sammons, P., Stobart, G., Kington, A. and Gu, Q. (2007) *Teachers Matter: Connecting Lives, Work and Effectiveness*. Berkshire: McGraw Hill.

Gravells, J. and Wallace, S. (2012) *Dial M for Mentor*. Norwich: Critical.

Howard, C., Burton, M. and Levermore, D. (2019) *Children's Mental Health and Emotional Well-being in Primary Schools* (2nd edn). Exeter: Learning Matters.

Jones, L., Tones, S. and Foulkes, G. (2018). Mentoring associate teachers in initial teacher education: the value of dialogic feedback. *International Journal of Mentoring and Coaching in Education*. 7(2), 127–38. https://doi.org/10.1108/IJMCE-07-2017-0051

Jones, L., Tones, S. and Foulkes, G. (2019) Exploring learning conversations between mentors and associate teachers in initial teacher education. *International Journal of Mentoring and Coaching in Education*. 8(2), 120–33.

Pask, R. and Joy, B. (2007) *Mentoring-Coaching: A Guide for Educational Professionals*. Berkshire: Oxford University Press.

REFERENCES

Barr, J. (2011) The relationship between teachers' empathy and perceptions of school culture. *Educational Studies*, 37(3). 365–9.

Beijaard, D., Meijer, P. and Verloop, N. (2004) 'Reconsidering Research on Teachers' Professional Identity'. *Teaching and Teacher Education*, 20(2), 107–28.

Blackmore, K., Howard, C. and Kington, A. (2018) Trainee teachers' experience of primary science teaching, and the perceived impact on their developing professional identity. *European Journal of Teacher Education*, 1–20. ISSN 0261-9768 Online.

Certo, J.L. (2005) Support, challenge, and the two way street: perceptions of a beginning second grade teacher and her quality mentor. *Journal of Early Childhood Teacher Education*, 26(1), 3–21.

Chun, J.U., Litzky, E.B., Sosik, J.J., Bechtold, D.C. and Godshalk, V.M. (2010) Emotional intelligence and trust in formal mentoring programs. *Group and Organization Management*, 35(4), 421–55.

Corradi, F. (1990) *The Other Side of Language*. New York: Routledge.

Department for Education (DfE) (2011) Teachers' standards: guidance for school leaders, school staff and governing bodies. Available at: https://assets.publishing.service.gov.uk/government/uploads/system/uploads/attachment_data/file/665520/Teachers__Standards.pdf (accessed 9 November 2018).

Dhillon, J. (2009) The role of social capital in sustaining partnership. *British Educational Research Journal*, 35(5), 687–704.

Gehrke, N. and Kay, R. (1984) The socialisation of beginning teachers through mentor-protégé relationships. *Journal of Teacher Education*, 3(21), 21–4.

Goleman, D. (1998) *Working with Emotional Intelligence*. London: Bloomsbury.

Hobson, A.J. and Malderez, A. (2013) 'Judgementoring and other threats to realizing the potential of school-based mentoring in teacher education'. *International Journal of Mentoring and Coaching in Education*, 2(2), 89–108.

Hobson, A.J., Ashby, P., Maderez, A. and Tomlinson, P. (2009) Mentoring beginning teachers: what we know and what we don't. *Teaching and Teacher Education*, 25, 207–16.

Hong, J. (2010) Pre-service and beginning teachers' professional identity and its relation to dropping out of the profession. *Teaching and Teacher Education*, 26(8), 1530–43.

Howard, C., Burton, M. and Levermore, D. (2019) *Children's Mental Health and Emotional Well-being in Primary Schools* (2nd edn). Exeter: Learning Matters.

Hudson, P. (2005) Mentor's personal attributes for enhancing mentees' primary science. *Teaching Science*. 51(2), 31–4.

Hudson, P. (2007) Examining mentors' practices for enhancing preservice teachers' pedagogical development in mathematics and science. *Mentoring and Tutoring*, 15(2), 201–17.

Hudson, P. (2013) Desirable attributes and practices for mentees: mentor teachers' expectations. *European Journal of Educational Research*, 2(3), 107–19.

Hudson, P. and Hudson, S. (2018) Mentoring preservice teachers: identifying tensions and possible solutions. *Teacher Development*, 22(1), 16–30.

Jordan, J.V. and Schwartz, H.L. (2018) Radical empathy in teaching. *New Directions for Teaching and Learning*,18(153). Available at https://onlinelibrary.wiley.com/doi/abs/10.1002/tl.20278 (accessed 15 May 2019).

Jones, L., Tones, S. and Foulkes, G. (2018) Mentoring associate teachers in initial teacher education: the value of dialogic feedback. *International Journal of Mentoring and Coaching in Education*, 7(2), 127–38. https://doi.org/10.1108/IJMCE-07-2017-0051

Jones, L., Tones, S. and Foulkes, G. (2019) Exploring learning conversations between mentors and associate teachers in initial teacher education. *International Journal of Mentoring and Coaching in Education*. 8(2), 120–33.

Kutsyuruba, B. and Walker, K. (2015) The role of trust in developing teacher leaders through early-career induction and mentoring programs. *Antistasis*, 5(1), 32–6.

Kyriacou, C., Kunc, R., Stephens, P. and Hultgren (2003) Student teacher' expectations of teaching as a career in England and Norway. *Educational Review*, 55(3), 255–63.

Lave, J. and Wenger, E. (1991) *Situated Learning: Legitimate Peripheral Participation*. Cambridge: Cambridge University Press.

Nahmad-Williams, L. (2013) Reflection, in Taylor, K. and Woolley, R., *Values and Vision in Primary Education*. Berkshire: Open University.

O'Sullivan, D. and Conway, P.F. (2016) Undewhelmed and playing it safe: newly qualified primary teachers' mentoring and probationary-related experiences during induction. *Irish Educational Studies*, 35(4), 403–20.

Pask, R. and Joy, B. (2007) *Mentoring-Coaching: A Guide for Educational Professionals*. Berkshire: Oxford University Press.

Shields, S. and Murray, M. (2017) Beginning teachers' perceptions of mentors and access to communities of practice. *International Journal of Mentoring and Coaching in Education*, 6(4), 317–31.

Stanulis, R.N. and Russell, D. (2000) 'Jumping in': trust and communication in mentoring student teachers. *Teacher and Teacher Education*, 16, 65–80.

Teaching Schools Council (2016) *National Standards for School-Based Initial Teacher Training (ITT) Mentors*. Available at https://assets.publishing.service.gov.uk/government/uploads/system/uploads/attachment_data/file/536891/Mentor_standards_report_Final.pdf (accessed 2 January 2019).

Timmerman, G. (2009) Teacher educators modelling their teachers? *European Journal of Teacher Education*, 32(3), 225–38.

Thomas, W. and Smith, A. (2009) *Coaching Solutions: Practical Ways to Improve Performance in Education*. London: Network Continuum.

Thornton, M. (1999) Reducing wastage among men student teachers in primary courses: a male club approach. *Journal for Education for Teaching*, 25(1), 41–53.

Wang, J. and Odell, S.J. (2002) Mentored learning to teach according to standards-based reforms. *Review of Educational Research*, 72(3), 481–546.

Wenger, E. 2000. Communities of practice and social learning systems. *Organization*, 7, 225–46.

Woolley, R. (2013) Values, in Taylor, K. and Woolley, R., *Values and Vision in Primary Education*. Berkshire: Open University.

3

STANDARD 2: TEACHING

CHAPTER OBJECTIVES

By the end of this chapter, you should be aware of a range of strategies which you might utilise in order to support your mentee:

- to form positive relationships with pupils and develop effective behaviour for learning strategies
- to access relevant subject and pedagogical knowledge
- to use educational research effectively
- to further develop their planning, teaching and assessment and reflect upon the impact it has on children's progress and achievement
- by giving them effective feedback on lessons.

MENTOR STANDARDS

This chapter supports the development of the following Mentor Standard (Teaching Schools Council, 2016, p.10):

Standard 2 – Teaching

Support trainees to develop their teaching practice in order to set high expectations of all pupils and to meet their needs.

INTRODUCTION

This chapter will outline what, on first reflection, would appear to be the most clearly defined of the roles of the mentor – that of a critical friend who will facilitate the further development of their mentee's teaching skills. It seems obvious that if school-based mentors are to enable their mentees to be successful, the newly qualified teacher needs to understand the 'nuts and bolts' of the learning and teaching process. Nevertheless, we know that learning and teaching are complex and despite the fact that the experienced teacher may initially make these processes look easy, there is subtlety and nuance to them. Consequently, this chapter will explore a diverse range of areas and you may find that giving yourself time to explore some of these in more depth by reading more widely might be effective. If you would like to further consider any of these areas of focus, suggestions for additional reading can be found at the end of this chapter.

SUPPORTING YOUR MENTEE TO DEVELOP EFFECTIVE BEHAVIOUR MANAGEMENT STRATEGIES

It is clear to any mentor who has worked closely with novice teachers that a confident approach to developing positive relationships with pupils, and skilfully managing their behaviour, are prerequisites of meeting a range of the Teachers' Standards. Frequently, it is Teachers' Standard 7 (DfE, 2011) that many inexperienced colleagues feel most anxious about when they start their career and sadly, for some, this is a factor in their decision to leave the teaching profession early. As Bennett (2017, p.12) states, 'Behaviour does not manage itself, except haphazardly,' so it is vital that a mentor can confidently support their mentee to have the teacher presence, knowledge and skills to be able to ensure a safe and productive learning environment from the outset.

As professionals, we know that authoritative teachers are most able to motivate students and have a positive impact on their learning (Vaaland, 2017). Consequently, it is clear that one of the simplest things that a mentor can do to enable their mentee to command respect and exude authority is to support them to understand the behaviour management systems within their school. We all feel more confident within an environment that we understand and feel comfortable in. Simply, this can be achieved by giving your mentee access to relevant policies and an opportunity for dialogue and the unravelling of the detail within. Each school is unique and the behavioural ethos is clearly contextualised. It would be easy for a new teacher to take an approach utilised within another setting and unwittingly cause difficulties for the wider school community. A 20-minute conversation which unpicks the rationale and salient features of the behaviour policy, whilst the early career teacher (ECT) highlights relevant sections and processes and clarifies any queries, is time well spent, not only specifically in regard to the issues discussed above, but also with regard to other key policies such as safeguarding.

Having considered that each school ethos is unique, it is wise to consider that all pupils are unique individuals too. We know that a detailed knowledge of the academic and personal attributes of our pupils will enable a more refined approach when considering classroom management. Accordingly, it is vital that the supportive mentor enables their mentee access to key records, planning and less formal information in a timely manner to allow a holistic understanding of the young people with whom they are engaging. By protecting some valuable time for the mentee to discuss individual pupils with the teacher who taught them previously, and sharing documents such as individual behaviour plans (IBPs), the new teacher will be better prepared to plan successful lessons which engage and challenge their students. This in turn will enable productive relationships to be fostered.

Although it is pertinent to remember that each teacher will bring their own values and a personal vision of what effective learning and teaching looks like, one approach which mentors might use to enable their mentee to reflect upon behaviour management techniques is demonstration or modelling. 'If you model yourself on someone, you copy the way that they do things, because you admire them and want to be like them' (Collins Dictionary (online), 2019). Trying to develop teachers in one's own image is not the most effective way of supporting new colleagues, however, particularly when they are early in their learning journey; the observation of a more experienced colleague may give the novice time to reflect upon and process their thoughts about effective teaching approaches. Snyder et al.'s (2012) wide-ranging review of childhood professional development highlights modelling as one effective approach. Mosley Wetzel et al. (2017) take the notion of simple modelling further by reflecting upon how retrospective video analysis, utilised within a coaching context, can be a powerful tool. This is a seemingly more radical approach to supporting professional development; however, modern technology is becoming an integral part of our lives with teachers readily utilising platforms such as Twitter to engage with online professional communities and communicate with their peers. Lofthouse and Birmingham (2010) found that the use of video to record lessons delivered by trainee teachers gave them a more nuanced perspective of their teaching and allowed them to engage more eagerly in reflective practice, which is fundamental to the ownership of Teachers' Standard 8 (DfE, 2011). With readily available tablets this is a simple yet powerful strategy which, with a consideration of data protection regulations, could transform the mentee's perceptions of a lesson. Alongside carefully managed coaching, structured questioning and opportunities to explore thoughts and reflections, technology can be a powerful tool for self-development where the modelling process is owned by the mentee themselves as they become their very own model to analyse and reflect upon. In order to add some structure to the post-video analysis, Chapter 7 will further explore reflection and offers models which could be utilised alongside this approach.

The best dialogue between the novice teacher and their mentor enables the novice to have ownership of their own professional development journey. One way in which this ownership can be facilitated is by the use of a personal, reflective journal. Zulfikar and Mujiburrahman (2018) consider that journals enable teachers to develop and enhance their pedagogy by increasing their awareness of aspects of their teaching. Nichols et al. (2017, p.419) explore the value of 'emotional episodes in shaping the nature of teachers' identities' and consider journals a valuable tool if supported with 'debriefing opportunities'. Larrivee (2008, p.88) develops this further when she contemplates the idea of 'a perpetual learning spiral'. Of course, this notion infers that it is impossible to ever perfect one's teaching and, for a novice, this reflection can be a liberating thought. In exploring that it is normal to expect 'Two steps forward one step backward' (Larrivee, 2008, p.93) the mentor might also exemplify their own 'bumpy road' to professional competency during mentoring discussions. This sharing of one's own professional journey, 'warts and all', is something that we should readily engage in as experienced colleagues. It is too easy for the novice teacher to assume that more experienced colleagues navigate their own career and professional development without challenge. Surely then, any strategy that demystifies the complexity of teaching and highlights a realistic viewpoint can only be a positive action.

A word of caution, however: there is no doubt that, if used well, a reflective journal can be a powerful tool, but it is vital not to add to the workload of your mentee. We know that in their first six years of teaching ECTs work more hours per week than more experienced teachers (DfE, 2019). Nonetheless, if kept focused and simple, a journal can pay dividends when exploited alongside time for pertinent discussion.

CASE STUDY: SAM

Sam is a newly qualified teacher who has successfully completed his first term in a Year 6 class within a large, urban Primary school. He has settled into life in school and feels strongly supported by his induction mentor, Andy.

Sam happily returns to school after the Christmas break and within two weeks finds that he has one or two pupils in his class who are displaying low-level disruptive behaviour. Coming from a sports coaching background,

(Continued)

(Continued)

Sam prides himself on having strong behaviour management and throughout all his school placements at university was praised for developing a positive learning environment. Andy hears confidentially from a colleague, whose classroom is next door to Sam's, that Sam has shouted at some of the children in his class who are becoming disruptive. In their weekly review meeting, Sam tells Andy that he is 'struggling' with the behaviour of three of the pupils within his class.

How should Andy further explore with Sam the challenges that he is facing?

Andy might suggest to Sam the use of a daily reflective journal to be completed over the course of a week. Sam might record how the children have behaved each day and any thoughts he might have about triggers for the unacceptable behaviour – for example, who they are sitting next to, whether the lesson is pitched correctly, if the behaviour worsens at certain parts of the day (after lunchtime break). At the end of the week, Andy and Sam can discuss the findings and consider if there are ways to reduce the triggers. The diary can then be utilised for a further week with any changes recorded and further discussed.

KEY REFLECTIONS

- How might you enable your mentee to reflect upon what factors 'trigger' challenging pupil behaviour?

- Might you consider whether your mentee would value the use of a reflective journal?

- Which particular aspects of best practice – for instance, effectively pitched and differentiated lesson planning, good use of time during transitions and non-verbal behavioural techniques – might be usefully modelled for your mentee? When and by whom?

- Might retrospective video analysis be helpful for your mentee? How could this be utilised to best effect and what might be the barriers to its effective use?

ENABLING ACCESS TO EXPERT SUBJECT AND PEDAGOGICAL KNOWLEDGE AND OBSERVATION OF BEST PRACTICE

It is evident that the notion of subject knowledge and curriculum are currently key foci within educational circles due, in no small part, to the scrutiny of Ofsted and another new framework for inspection. Spielman (2018) considers the importance of a comprehensive and confident knowledge of curricular subjects. It is clear that it is challenging to engage in the process of learning and teaching without an assured appreciation and ownership of subject knowledge. This is true for colleagues within the Secondary sector who have a very complex understanding of their specialist subject. When considering Primary-based colleagues we know there is increased complication due to the range of curricular areas taught.

Evens et al. (2015, p.245) consider Shulman's definition of his own seminal notion of pedagogical content knowledge (PCK), 'that special amalgam of content and pedagogy that is uniquely the province of teachers, their own special form of professional understanding'. Abell (2008, p.1414) further reflects that it would be unwise to recommend that teaching professionals acquire what she calls 'a bag of tricks based on a set of general pedagogical strategies'. Instead, she recommends that teachers consider how they might ensure that they cultivate a font of knowledge, accounting for the unique context in which their students learn, applying this to the specific challenges that each learner faces. So, how does the teacher mentor support their newly qualified mentee to access expert subject and pedagogical knowledge?

The DfE (2016) expects that quality professional development in schools should involve a widespread ethos of scholarship with a commitment from all colleagues to support each other to grow professionally. Knight (2017, p.854), when considering student teachers in particular, also wants us to reflect upon the community of expertise within a school and the possibilities that this might offer for subject knowledge development. He sees the mentor as the 'gatekeeper to wider sources of learning within the school'. He asks us to consider how the induction processes for colleagues joining a school community might be utilised to highlight the ways in which the school works as a broader learning community. There is an opportunity here for a mentor to consult with senior colleagues in a timely manner to protect induction time and negotiate a succinct, yet clear, learning entitlement plan for their mentee. If this can be agreed upon before the ECT starts their induction year, it can become a strategic, yet flexible, way of enabling a range of powerful continuing professional development (CPD) opportunities.

As part of a learning entitlement plan, the simplest yet one of the most powerful CPD opportunities which can enhance one's PCK is co-planning with a subject specialist. As time progresses, if managed well, this 1:1 specialist support should become less directed and more of a joint endeavour. Pylman (2016, p.52) considers Pearson and Gallagher (1983), who discuss a gradual transference as the less experienced colleague reflects upon how a series of learning opportunities has been scaffolded to enable maximum progress for pupils. Over time, techniques, strategies and carefully crafted progressions become more easily planned by the novice without additional support.

Effectively managing the precious time for co-planning is vital and Pylman (2016) asks us to consider a useful scaffold to structure this opportunity wisely.

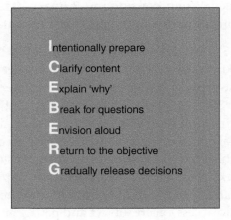

Intentionally prepare

Clarify content

Explain 'why'

Break for questions

Envision aloud

Return to the objective

Gradually release decisions

Figure 3.1   The co-planning ICEBERG (Pylman, 2016, p.46)

Within the 'iceberg' model, Pylman suggests careful preparation for the co-planning session so that the mentee's key learning target can be supported. She recommends that concepts, content and misconceptions are explored and that the mentor (or mentee if they are taking the lead) should verbalise why they are making certain pedagogical decisions. The opportunity for the novice teacher to ask questions is vital alongside visualising of what might happen within the lesson by the colleague leading the planning. Finally, Pylman reflects that the lesson objective should be carefully considered.

CASE STUDY: SOFIA

Sofia is in the second term of her induction year and is teaching a Year 2 class in a two-form entry first school. She is hard-working and professional and is well liked by everyone. Sofia's mentor Emma has observed lessons in a range of subjects over the year and all of them have been effectively planned and supportive of good pupil progress.

Two weeks into the spring term, Sofia asks Emma if she would observe her teaching a phonics lesson, as this is a subject area in which she feels less confident. She would like some advice and values Emma as a critical friend.

Emma observes a phonics lesson in which the large majority of the children make no progress. It is clear that Sofia has not taken into account prior learning, there is little active engagement from the children and there is inaccurate pronunciation with the 'schwa' sound being modelled.

What might be the best way to further support Sofia's weak phonics knowledge?

It is positive that Sofia is aware (as she asked Emma to observe and give her feedback) that this is a subject area that she is less confident teaching so she may feel optimistic about opportunities for honest dialogue and support. Initially, Emma might arrange for Sofia to plan for a well-pitched phonics lesson with direction from the Literacy co-ordinator during her NQT release time. The Literacy co-ordinator might then deliver this lesson whilst Sofia observes and focuses on the progress that is made by the children and the methods of delivery. A post-lesson discussion could then consider Sofia's reflections and the following week this planning process might be repeated with Sofia delivering the co-planned session. Emma and Sofia might discuss what has been learned at a planned review meeting.

It is important to note, however, that if the issue is a lack of phonics subject knowledge per se, Sofia will need plenty of time to be able to access online support materials, phonics webinars or face-to-face CPD. Co-planning will enable her to utilise a relevant lesson structure and consider how best to consider prior knowledge before planning, but, as mentioned above, confident delivery depends on a nuanced understanding which takes time to develop.

KEY REFLECTIONS

- For which particular subject areas might your mentee benefit from additional support with planning? How might you prioritise these?

(Continued)

(Continued)

- What might be the best way to facilitate the time for an experienced colleague to support your mentee with lesson planning?

- How might you use the iceberg model (Pylman, 2016) during a lesson planning support session for your mentee?

SUPPORTiNG YOUR MENTEE TO DEVELOP APPROACHES TO TEACHiNG AND ASSESSMENT

The burden on Primary teachers to raise standards of learning and teaching, in order to have the greatest impact on pupil progress and achievement, has been relentless since attainment targets and levels were introduced with the national curriculum under the Education Reform Act from 1989 (HMSO, 1988). This was further enhanced when standard attainment tests (SATs) were developed by the government from 1991. Consequently, when Paul Black and Dylan Wiliam (1998) asked teacher professionals to explore *Inside the Black Box* the profession as a whole had been grappling with finding the most simple and cohesive way to utilise effective assessment techniques and strategies for more than a decade. The publication of the Final report of the Commission on Assessment without Levels (DfE, 2015), although seen by most as a positive development, added to this animated discourse and further complicated the national assessment landscape. Thus, it would be unwise for me to try to simplify this intricate landscape within one chapter to create Abell's 'bag of tricks' (Abell, 2008, p.1414). Instead, I shall consider a vehicle through which teaching and assessment per se can become a focus for development: that of 'lesson study'.

The notion of lesson study has long been considered by educationalists since its growth from what Elliot (2019, p.176) describes as its 'methodological roots in Japanese Primary schools' to its wider use across countries within the Western world. Elliot (2019) appreciates that there is not merely one definition of lesson study, but contemplates the breadth of research highlighting teachers as researchers who collaborate to plan, deliver, observe and reflect upon learning. On its website, the Teacher Development Trust (TDT) also outlines this approach to professional development, but cautions about ensuring that it is implemented sensitively and with consideration for teacher workload.

Dudley (2013, p.109) bemoans the fact that 'the presence of a fellow professional in one's classroom is associated with performance management or inspection'.

For the ECT this 'additional other' within the room, who is a critical friend who supports and encourages but also may well be assessing progress, can create tension. Dudley (2013) highlights that teachers learn best when they work within a safe environment, collaborating with colleagues. For the novice teacher in particular, to engage as a professional within an enquiry-based approach with a group of more experienced colleagues can normalise observation and remove the intense focus away from their own personal pedagogy. Enabling teachers to understand their pupils learning holistically, and in more depth, is something that Dudley (2013) celebrates as revolutionary and he helpfully shares the model shown in Figure 3.2.

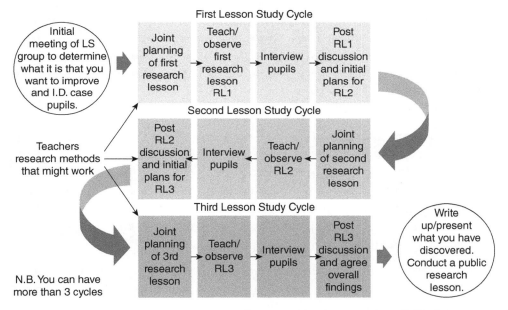

Figure 3.2   First lesson study cycle (Dudley, 2013, p.108)

Using the model in Figure 3.2, focusing specifically on aspects of learning and teaching such as the impact of questioning on pupil learning or the development of effective mini-plenaries to address misconceptions could have a transformational effect on the understanding of formative assessment of the novice. As the model evidences, this is a cyclical process with opportunities for colleagues to reflect on a specific aspect of learning. As a collaborative technique, it also allows the more experienced colleagues within the group to utilise another lens through which to view learning, so is truly a symbiotic approach to staff development.

Since its establishment in 2017, the Chartered College of Teaching (CCoT, 2017), within its mission statement, has communicated that it wants to 'be the conduit to a more evidence-informed profession'. Lesson study, supported by easily accessible and relatively inexpensive resources, such as the peer reviewed journals, online learning platform and peer networks provided by the Chartered College of Teaching, is certainly an approach for the ECT mentor to consider for their mentee.

CASE STUDY: SUNETRA

Sunetra is an NQT in the final term of her induction year who has been responsible for a large mixed-age class of Year 3/4 children in a small, four-class rural Primary school. The school has a pupil intake of 35 per cent of pupils with SEND and 45 per cent of children who are eligible for pupil premium. Sunetra's class has the largest percentage of children with SEND in the school. Joe, her mentor, has seen Sunetra grow in confidence throughout her first year of teaching, and her commitment to the pupils and wider life of the school has been evident to everyone. However, from the outset, Sunetra has found the mixed-ability nature of the class challenging.

Joe enabled Sunetra to have a half-day non-contact time during the first term to seek advice from the well-respected school SENCo about how to plan for removal of barriers to learning for the children with learning difficulties. This had an impact on Sunetra's confidence with planning and, consequently, the progress of the children with significant barriers to learning. The following term, Joe arranged for his mentee to co-plan with expert colleagues in Mathematics and English during her weekly NQT time.

A whole school lesson study approach could further support Sunetra's understanding of assessment during her second year of teaching and also become a professional development tool for the whole school.

KEY REFLECTIONS

- When and how might a lesson study approach best be implemented? Which colleagues could be involved? How might senior leadership colleagues support the timing and resourcing of this approach?

- What might be the focus of an 'enquiry question' (TDT) and how might it be crafted collaboratively?

GIVING YOUR MENTEE CONSTRUCTIVE, CLEAR AND TIMELY FEEDBACK AFTER OBSERVATIONS

Learning walks or teacher observations? Whatever the terminology, the process of an additional other (frequently a senior colleague) reflecting upon the effectiveness of the learning and teaching process within a classroom is not a new construct. For years, observing teachers has been a pursuit that has been exploited for a range of reasons: from Ofsted inspectors gauging the overall effectiveness of a school to a Science lead in search of ascertaining what support is needed for colleagues to senior staff monitoring for performance management or disciplinary procedures. Being observed can be a stressful process for any teacher and a reason for this is the perceived lack of ownership of the process. ECTs in particular may feel vulnerable due to an internal pressure to 'deliver' or, even more worryingly, 'perform' a lesson which they view as perfect. It is vital for a mentor to agree with their mentee, before they complete an observation, that the rationale for the observation is to offer professional development support within a collegiate approach. Additionally, agreeing an area of focus beforehand allows the novice to fully reflect and emphasises a specific aspect of pedagogy rather than a 'skimming of the surface' of a wider aspect of their practise.

Archer et al. (2016) consider the dynamism of the classroom which adds complexity to the effectiveness of observation. Moreover, they ask that we consider how our own values of learning and teaching impact upon our interpretation of what we observe. Fruitful dialogue facilitating precise and meaningful feedback is the aspiration, so how might a mentor achieve this challenging goal in the midst of such a complex task? Certainly, it will involve the use of two-way learning conversation given that such an approach is more directive in its nature (Jones et al., 2019). As they indicate, the value of two-way learning conversations may be found in the co-construction of ideas linked to challenges between mentor and mentee. As they go onto note, such an approach may also help to build up a trusting and supportive relationship, as outlined in Chapter 2.

O'Leary and Wood (2017) urge that we do not merely observe but, alongside observation, explore and contemplate a range of complementary evidence over time. This may also include university-based mentor support in the form of a dialogic conversation. Thus, the notion of 'constructive, clear and timely feedback' (Teaching Schools Council, 2016, p.12) becomes a rather more complex and less linear process. Accordingly, the good mentor ensures that an adequate amount of time is protected, reasonably soon after a lesson observation, to enable an effective outcome.

In order to navigate this complex landscape, Lofthouse et al. (2010, pp.62–3) suggest the following coaching dimensions which might prove to be an effective resource to frame discussion for the busy mentor: subject matter, initiation, stimulus, tone, scale, time, interaction function. Additionally, they share a range of 'interaction functions' which enable us to consider each dialogic 'turn' in the conversation.

CASE STUDY: WERONIKA

Weronika is due to observe her mentee Jacob tomorrow afternoon. They have agreed the date and time of the observation and both have protected an hour after school for a post-observation discussion. She considers the coaching dimensions (Lofthouse et al., 2010) the day before in order to prepare for her post-observation dialogue and makes brief planning notes.

SUBJECT MATTER

Jacob has asked that the focus for the observation should be the effectiveness of his use of questioning as a formative assessment tool.

INITIATION AND STIMULUS

Weronika would like Jacob to initially share with her how effective he felt his use of questioning was. As a stimulus, she wants him to use evidence from the children's books and his own lesson planning to support his reflections.

TONE

Jacob has shown Weronika that he is committed and hard-working and they have a trusting, professional relationship. Weronika expects this to be a positive discussion and reflects that she will continue to adopt a positive or neutral tone.

SCALE

It has been agreed that the observation will be for approximately 30 minutes. Weronika is interested to see whether there will be a particular 'episode' or 'critical incident' which will influence the scope of the dialogue.

TIME

Making links between his previous, current and future practice is something that Weronika has seen Jacob do consistently well throughout his post-observation discussions. She wonders, will he be able to see these links tomorrow with regard to his use of questioning?

INTERACTION FUNCTION

As an experienced coach, Weronika considers the range of ways that language might be used in the coaching discussion: question, evaluation, summary, acceptance, challenge, context, generalisation, clarification, new idea, justification, explanation, continuity, dissonance. She considers how to enable Jacob to have opportunities to justify his actions and also how she might specifically summarise aspects of the discussion.

KEY REFLECTIONS

- How might the mentor and mentee decide upon the focus for the observation? What factors might they specifically take into account?

- How long might the observation last? What factors will influence this?

- What 'stimulus' or resources might the mentee bring to enable a purposeful dialogue?

SUPPORTING EARLY CAREER TEACHERS TO RESOLVE IN-SCHOOL ISSUES

For the novice teacher, a new school community can be a 'spider's web' of personal and professional challenges. Within the day there are a multitude of social situations to navigate: morning discussions with parents about homework, conversations about behaviour management with lunchtime supervisors, planning deliberations with teaching assistants and staff meeting reflections with senior leaders add to the complexity of daily life, and that is before interactions with pupils have been considered. The best teachers steer their way through this social minefield with empathy and use their experience to show the school community that they are both caring and capable. The challenge for the novice teacher is to quickly familiarise themselves with the systems within the school in addition to gauging the personalities of the people with whom they work. Much of the time, their desire to make a good impression and integrate into the school community means that the induction period passes by reasonably smoothly.

For the experienced mentor, many issues faced by their mentee might be counteracted if, as mentioned above, there is dedicated time to explore systems, processes and expectations in the first few weeks. Similarly, a wise mentor will promote regular discussion and urge their mentee to communicate in a timely manner, sharing challenges they face and helping to explore practical solutions if the mentee is unsure about how to proceed. Eliahoo (2016, p.311) believes that solutions should be 'mulled over' and reflects that, for the mentor this takes 'time and energy, as well as skill, experience and judgement'. She cautions that inconsequential issues could quickly intensify with damaging consequences should a mentor not intervene in a timely way and that regular discussion will enable a mentor to predict potential conflicts more readily.

Struyve et al. (2016) contemplate the importance of social connectedness and the social infrastructure in which ECTs are placed on teacher identity and well-being. They suggest that it is vital to remember that mentoring can also be found via informal sources such as one's peers and does not only come from those in a formal role. A mentor might, therefore, facilitate what Struyve et al. (2016, p.214) call an 'informal social ecosystem of support' for their mentee. This broadens the capacity for support and allows other colleagues to share their own perspectives and model professional expectations, quickly giving the novice an enhanced understanding of the values of individuals within the community and less opportunity to inadvertently generate a misunderstanding.

Drawing the chapter to a close, it would seem pertinent to mention the importance of positive mental health for one's mentee and the issue of work–life balance is one that is indelibly linked with the notion of the effective management of in-school issues. We all reflect more clearly, toil more thoughtfully, make fewer errors and utilise a positive mindset if we have had opportunities for adequate rest and relaxation. Hobson and Maxwell (2017) urge school leaders to maintain their duty of care to ECTs and to generate an optimal environment for teacher welfare. Practical suggestions about how to best use time in the school day and manage competing priorities would be positive to explore with your mentee in addition to ensuring that their workload is manageable. Within the current national environment where the Early Career Framework is imminently on the horizon, we look forward to a supportive national direction of travel for all novice teacher colleagues and their wonderfully supportive mentors too.

KEY REFLECTIONS

This is a final reflective question to consider now you have read this chapter.

What aspects of professional development and support might be included in a learning entitlement plan and how might you liaise with senior colleagues to facilitate this for your mentee?

CHAPTER SUMMARY

- The careful development of a learning entitlement plan is a strategic way to design the professional development opportunities offered to a novice teacher.

- It is imperative to protect time early in the induction year for a mentor to share the detail of school policies and processes with their mentee.

- Timely access to pupil records can facilitate a smooth transition into planning and assessment for an NQT at the start of their induction.

- Technology such as video recording, enhanced by focused dialogue, can enable an ECT to reflect upon the nuances of their own pedagogical approach.

- Careful use of a journal can empower a novice teacher to take ownership of their learning.

- Co-planning opportunities, with a more experienced colleague, can be influential for the development of an NQT's pedagogical subject knowledge if the sessions are well-structured.

- Although initially time-consuming to plan and complex to manage, lesson study is a powerful strategy for enabling teachers to consider the impact of their approaches on their pupils' learning.

- The ways in which language is framed within a coaching context can have a significant impact upon whether a post-observation discussion is fruitful.

SELF-AUDIT QUESTIONS

- How might you further develop your ability to frame language to impact positively upon a coaching conversation?

- How might you manage your limited time for mentoring support to enable your mentee to have the best possible opportunity for discussion and reflection?

SUGGESTED ADDITIONAL READING

Hudson, P. and Hudson, S. (2018) Mentoring preservice teachers: identifying tensions and possible resolutions. *Teacher Development*, 22(1), 16–30. Available at doi: 10.1080/13664530.2017.1298535

Lofthouse, R. (2018) *International Journal of Mentoring and Coaching in Education*, 7(3), 24–60.

Shulman, L. (1987) Knowledge and teaching: foundations of the new reform. *Harvard Educational Review*, 57(1), 1–23. Available at doi: 10.17763/haer.57.1.j463w79r56455411

REFERENCES

Abell, S.K. (2008) Twenty years later: does pedagogical content knowledge remain a useful idea? *International Journal of Science Education*, 30(10), 1405–16.

Archer, J., Cantrell, S., Holtzman, S.L., Joe, J.N., Tocci, C.M. and Wood, J. (2016) *Better Feedback for Better Teaching: A Practical Guide to Improving Classroom Observations* New York: John Wiley & Sons.

Bennett, T. (2017) *Creating a Culture: How School Leaders can Optimise Behaviour*. Available at https://assets.publishing.service.gov.uk/government/uploads/system/uploads/attachment_data/file/602487/Tom_Bennett_Independent_Review_of_Behaviour_in_Schools.pdf (accessed 20 June 2019).

Black, P. and Wiliam, D. (1998) *Inside the Black Box: Raising Standards Through Classroom Assessment*. London: King's College.

Collins Dictionary. Available at https://www.collinsdictionary.com/dictionary/english/model (accessed 20 June 2019).

Department for Education (DfE) (2011) Teachers' Standards: Guidance for School Leaders, School Staff and Governing Bodies. Available at: https://assets.publishing.service.gov.uk/government/uploads/system/uploads/attachment_data/file/665520/Teachers__Standards.pdf (accessed 16 July 2019).

Department for Education (2015) Final report of the Commission on Assessment without Levels. Available at https://assets.publishing.service.gov.uk/government/uploads/system/uploads/attachment_data/file/483058/Commission_on_Assessment_Without_Levels_-_report.pdf (accessed 29 June 2019).

Department for Education (2016) Standard for teachers' professional development. Available at https://assets.publishing.service.gov.uk/government/uploads/system/uploads/attachment_data/file/537030/160712_-_PD_standard.pdf (accessed 9 August 2019).

Department for Education (2019) Reducing workload: supporting teachers in the early stages of their career. *Advice for school leaders, induction tutors, mentors and appropriate bodies*. Available at https://assets.publishing.service.gov.uk/government/uploads/system/uploads/attachment_data/file/786178/Advice_for_ECTs_update.pdf (accessed 15 July 2019).

Dudley, P. (2013) Teacher learning in lesson study: what interaction-level discourse analysis revealed about how teachers utilised imagination, tacit knowledge of teaching and fresh evidence of pupils learning, to develop practice knowledge and so enhance their pupils' learning. *Teaching and Teacher Education*, 34, 107–21. Available at https://reader.elsevier.com/reader/sd/pii/S0742051X13000735?token=A32278664128DB4A504C1B6EFF256258885A5E6688046F6965B1582A617D76D938CAC11D5EED7F677C30B782158F1E43 (accessed 16 July 2019).

Eliahoo, R. (2016) An analysis of beginning mentors' critical incidents in English post-compulsory education: navigating stormy waters. *International Journal of Mentoring and Coaching in Education*, 5(4), 304–17. Available at doi: 10.1108/IJMCE-08-2016-0060 (accessed 20 July 2019).

Elliot, J. (2019) What is lesson study? *European Journal of Education*, 54(2).

Evens, M., Elen, J. and Depaepe, F. (2015) Developing pedagogical content knowledge: lessons learned from intervention studies. *Education Research International*, 1–23. Available at https://search.proquest.com/docview/1706167642?pq-origsite=summon&accountid=15133 (accessed 9 August 2019).

Her Majesty's Stationary Office (1988) Education Reform Act. Available at http://www.legislation.gov.uk/ukpga/1988/40/pdfs/ukpga_19880040_en.pdf (accessed 9 August 2019).

Hobson, A.J. and Maxwell, B. (2017) Supporting and inhibiting the well-being of early career secondary school teachers: extending self-determination theory. *British Educational Research Journal*, 43(1), 168–91.

Jones, L., Tones, S. and Foulkes, G. (2019) Exploring learning conversations between mentors and associate teachers in initial teacher education. *International Journal of Mentoring and Coaching in Education*, 8(2), 120–33.

Knight, R. (2017) The subject and the setting: re-imagining opportunities for primary teachers' subject knowledge development on school-based teacher education courses. *Teachers and Teaching*, 23(7), 843–58.

Larrivee, B. (2008) Meeting the challenge of preparing reflective practitioners. *The New Educator*, 4(2), 87–106. Available at doi: 10.1080/15476880802014132 (accessed 14 July 2019).

Lofthouse, R. and Birmingham, P. (2010) The camera in the classroom: video- recording as a tool for professional development of student teachers. *TEAN Journal*, 1(2). Available at http://ojs.cumbria.ac.uk/index.php/tean/article/view/59/70 (accessed 4 April 2019).

Lofthouse, R. et al. (2010) Improving coaching: evolution not revolution. *CfBT Education Trust*. Available at https://dera.ioe.ac.uk/2085/7/improving-coaching_Redacted.pdf (accessed 19 July 2019).

Mosley Wetzel, M., Maloch, B. and Hoffman, J.V. (2017), Retrospective video analysis: a reflective tool for teachers and teacher educators. *The Reading Teacher*, 70(5), 533–42.

Nichols, S.L., Schutz, P.A., Rodgers, K. and Bilica, K. (2017) Early career teachers' emotion and emerging teacher identities. *Teachers and Teaching*, 23(4), 406–21. Available at doi: 10.1080/13540602.2016.1211099 (accessed 15 July 2019).

O'Leary, M. and Wood, P. (2017) Performance over professional learning and the complexity puzzle: lesson observation in England's further education sector. *Professional Development in Education*, 43(4). Available at doi: 10.1080/19415257.2016.1210665 (accessed 19 July 2019).

Pearson, P.D., and Gallagher, M. (1983) The instruction of reading comprehension. *Contemporary Educational Psychology*, 8, 317–44. Available at doi: 10.1016/0361-476X(83)90019-X (accessed 15 July 2019).

Pylman, S. (2016) Reflecting on talk: a mentor teacher's gradual release in co-planning. *The New Educator*, 12(1), 48–66. Available at doi: 10.1080/1547688X.2015.1113347 (accessed 15 July 2019).

Snyder, P., Hemmeter, M.L., Meeker, K.A., Kinder, K., Pasia, C. and McLaughlin, T. (2012) Characterizing key features of the early childhood professional development literature. *Infants and Young Children*, 25, 188–22. Available at doi: 10.1097/IYC.0b013e31825a1ebf (accessed 9 August 2019).

Spielman, A. (2018) HMCI commentary: curriculum and the new education inspection framework. Available at https://www.gov.uk/government/speeches/hmci-commentary-curriculum-and-the-new-education-inspection-framework (accessed 20 June 2019).

Struyve, C., Daly, A., Vandecandelaere, M., Meredith, C., Hannes, K. et al. (2016) More than a mentor: the role of social connectedness in early career and experienced teachers' intention to leave. *Journal of Professional Capital and Community*. Available at doi: 10.1108/JPCC-01-2016-0002 (accessed 20 July 2019).

Teaching Schools Council (2016) *National Standards for School-Based Initial Teacher Training (ITT) Mentors*. Available at https://assets.publishing.service.gov.uk/government/uploads/system/uploads/attachment_data/file/536891/Mentor_standards_report_Final.pdf (accessed 16 July 2019).

The Chartered College of Teaching (2017) Mission statement. Available at https://chartered.college/vision-and-mission (accessed 16 July 2019).

Vaaland, G.S. (2017) Back on track: approaches to managing highly disruptive school classes. *Cogent Education*, 4, 1396656. Available at doi: 10.1080/2331186X.2017.1396656 (accessed 20 June 2019).

Zulfikar, T. and Mujiburrahman (2018) Understanding own teaching: becoming reflective teachers through reflective journals. *Reflective Practice*, 19(1), 1–13.

4

STANDARD 3: PROFESSIONALISM

CHAPTER OBJECTIVES

By the end of this chapter you should be aware of:

- how teaching as a profession is defined
- the important position you hold as both a role model and a school mentor
- the role of professional relationships
- how in your role as a school mentor you can support the development of trainee teachers and early career teachers.

MENTOR STANDARDS

Whilst this chapter addresses aspects of all of the school-based ITT Mentor Standards (Teaching Schools Council, 2016, p.12), there is specific reference to Standard 3 – Professionalism:

Set high expectations and induct the trainee to understand their role and responsibilities as a teacher.

Within the context of professionalism, the important role of a school mentor is recognised and has recently become a priority for the government, with the introduction of the school-based Mentor Standards (Teaching Schools Council, 2016). Building on the Mentor Standards, this chapter examines the way the role has evolved whilst considering how professionalism underpins the practice of mentoring trainees and early career entrants to the teaching profession.

iNTRODUCTiON

This chapter will explore what is understood by the term 'professionalism' in teaching and, more specifically, has a focus upon the professional role of a mentor. This is of importance as we examine what constitutes professionalism and what it means to hold a professional standing in school and in society. The Mentor Standards (Teaching Schools Council, 2016) provide a baseline by stating the minimum requirements for school mentors who support ITT. This chapter sets out how the professionalism of school mentors underpins these standards.

PERSPECTiVES OF PROFESSiONALiSM

The definition of teacher professionalism is complex and there is a vagueness about how professionalism is understood (Sachs, 2003; Eraut, 1994). This continues to be a source of debate: 'Indeed, lack of consensus over the meaning of professionalism is widely acknowledged' (Evans, 2011, p.854). However, Crook (2008) suggests that: 'the application of historical perspectives confirms professionalism to be an artificial construct, with ever-changing and always contested definitions' (p.23).

Professionalism has a history which is important, and over time the meaning of professionalism has changed (Holroyd, cited in Bourke et al., 2015). Whitty (2008) highlights how this idea of change applies to the standing a teacher holds in society and says that teaching has not held the same professional status as some traditional occupations, such as those in law or in the medical field. This is because teachers have not been left to manage their own matters in relation to teaching but have been regulated by government interventions. Teaching as a professional organisation has a past which has shaped it, but it has also been constrained from being under successive government control. Eraut reminds us that the teaching profession has 'had some difficulty in articulating a distinctive knowledge base, and ha[s] also suffered from being under much greater government control' (1994, p.3). This has been noticeable since the 1970s with teacher professionalism being held to account through changes to the curriculum and assessment including the introduction of the National Curriculum, national tests and target setting. So, with teachers and schools having greater accountability and government policies placed upon them the nature of teacher professionalism changed. It was now defined by the government in its Green Paper (DfEE,1998) as one that accepts accountability, makes decisions based on evidence of what works, works collaboratively with school colleagues and accepts that outside organisations can make valuable contributions to ensure the school is effective. Within these changes it was noted how training, recruitment and leadership would be important in modernising the teaching profession (DfEE, 1998). This represented a huge shift in the nature of teacher professionalism, highlighted by the DfEE (1998), which stated that:

> *the time has long gone when isolated, unaccountable professionals make curriculum and pedagogical decisions alone, without reference to the outside world.* (1998, p.14)

Schools are constantly changing and adapting, especially in response to policy changes. Wilkins suggests that it may have been easier to shape professionalism in the past, when there was less direction from the government:

> *The old professions grew their structures and identities in this way, in the days when governments were less bothered about regulation.* (2013, p.11)

The introduction of the Teachers' Standards in September 2012 (DfE, 2011) set a baseline for the conduct and practice of teachers, formally acknowledging a code which suggests a form of unity for education professionals. Evans (2011) further confirms that the Teachers' Standards 'collectively represent the professionalism that the government introducing them wants its teachers to manifest' (p.854). The introduction of the National Standards for school-based ITT mentors (Teaching Schools Council, 2016) offers an opportunity to review the reputation of school-based mentors. Magee (2017) suggests it is a chance to reaffirm the view that mentoring others is a skilled 'profession within a profession' (Lofthouse and Hall, 2014). This is because certain characteristics are needed specifically to fulfil a mentor's role. Consequently, Magee (2017) suggests this presents an opening where school-based mentors can be recruited to the role as these colleagues would be deemed to hold the necessary characteristics and skills. There is further discussion, later in this book, about the professional qualities of a mentor, which merit greater appreciation in relation to the valuable role of school-based mentors.

CHARACTERISTICS OF A PROFESSION

It could be said that teaching has less power than other 'ideal' professions, such as law, and it has been described as a 'semi-profession' (Eraut, 1997). The term 'semi-profession' grew out of the public sector and educational growth, which recognised that this occupation did not exhibit the traits that other formal professions portrayed, such as practitioners who work under strict ethical codes and where training is controlled through a professional body. Millerson (1964) defined specific characteristics of a profession and recognised that some traits appear realistic whilst others may seem restrictive. Amongst the essential traits, Millerson concludes, the following are considered important:

> *theoretical knowledge, training and education, passing a test, code of conduct, service is for the public good and the profession is organised.* (1964, p.4)

Whilst being helpful, because these characteristics and traits provide some understanding of what it means to be a professional, it also suggests a certain ambiguity. Eraut suggests that a definition of professional traits has not made it any easier to characterise professionalism, but rather it has served to highlight the characteristics of 'powerful professions which others seek to emulate' (1994, p.1). Contributing to the discussion, Watt (2014) proposed that Tristram Hunt, Labour Shadow Education Secretary, had further ideas to, 'raise the standard of the teaching profession'. One idea to empower the teaching profession is through teachers being licensed which, it is suggested, will place the professionalism of teachers in a stronger position:

This is about growing the profession. This is about believing that teachers have this enormous importance. Just like lawyers and doctors, they should have the same professional standing which means relicensing themselves. (Watt, 2014)

Teaching is the third most trusted profession, with nurses and doctors outperforming them, as the public trust these top-performing professions to tell the truth (George, 2018).

PROFESSIONAL KNOWLEDGE AND EXPERTISE

The label 'professional' is associated with having a body of knowledge (Etzioni, 1969) and expertise (Schön, 1983). Schön describes expertise as having expert knowledge and being able to apply that knowledge to problem-solving situations. When an expert solves problems they develop further expertise and this is a process (Tsui, 2009). When applied to a school mentor, the acceptance of being an expert in the field of education is aligned to years of practice and experience in the classroom. So the importance of being able to articulate why, alongside how, teaching is carried out becomes really important. In your role as a mentor you will find yourself explaining to a less experienced teacher the reasoning behind the pedagogy (Tsui, 2009). In this way you are able to draw on your expertise and knowledge.

KEY REFLECTIONS

- How would you define the professional role of a mentor?
- How is professionalism demonstrated through a mentor's qualities and skills?
- How does the mentor's attitude make a difference to how their role is perceived?

THE MENTOR AS A ROLE MODEL

In your role as a school-based mentor, you take on a responsibility to share your experiences and expertise in the field of education with a range of other less experienced colleagues to support their learning. Being a positive role model can be defined as someone who has influence, who displays knowledge and to whom others look to for advice. You may well remember, as a child, the teacher who inspired you and was a role model. How would you describe that teacher? We could say that a role model is someone that others aspire to be like, that they look up to and respect. As outlined in the Teachers' Standards Part Two (DfE, 2011, p.14), Teachers uphold public trust in the profession and maintain high standards of ethics and behaviour within and outside school.

As a mentor and as a role model you are an inspiration to others: you lead by example and uphold the trust of colleagues through your general disposition. Your commitment and drive is supportive to the mentee, who benefits from this relationship. With a growing concern over high dropout rates by early career teachers, mentoring could be considered as a response that may help to identify and address issues in a bid to retain good teachers (Heikkinen et al., 2018). Yet it is not a position to which all teachers are naturally suited or drawn. The mentor's role is multifarious, with mentors taking on a range of different roles (Cain, 2009); the role suits those deemed to be suitably qualified, an elite group. Kemmis et al. (2014) suggest that mentoring is carried out for different purposes, but essentially they consider a mentor to have a relationship with a less experienced colleague which Aspfors and Fransson (2015) say is ongoing over a long time span. Hudson (2013) comments that there are benefits of this role as it offers a professional development opportunity for mentors as they reflect on new ideas, develop their own skills and explain pedagogical practices.

It is important to remember that the relationship between you and the mentee does not exist in a vacuum and there are many factors that will impact upon it. This includes external factors such as how the role of a mentor is viewed within a school, the time to carry out the role and expectations from government directives (Bourke et al., 2015). Additionally, the mentor or the mentee may be having a difficult day, unexpected situations may crop up, there could be time challenges or personal issues. These are just a few things that could have an impact upon how you and the mentee work together. The part that feelings play in how the mentee responds to you should not be underestimated. Inexperienced teachers can be in danger of feeling anxious and in need of reassurance that they are doing well whilst they are in the transitional stage of their career (Cain, 2009). Having an awareness of any external challenges will support you to manage your own feelings too. It will help you to maintain a balance as you juggle the many aspects of upholding your position as a mentor and a role model. In the case study that follows, we explore the feelings of a new teacher and some possible support strategies.

CASE STUDY: MAX

Max is teaching in a Year 4 class with 28 pupils and works with a full-time teaching assistant (TA). The TA has worked at the school for over ten years and lives within the locality of the school; she therefore knows many of the families whose children attend the school. Max has become increasingly worried about his relationship with the TA and has started to feel undermined by her – she recently told him she will only work with a certain group of children in the class. Max feels uncomfortable about responding to the TA and is unsure how to effectively deploy this member of the support staff. He does not want to upset the TA, but is aware that one of his leadership roles as a teacher is to effectively deploy support staff. He asks for your advice.

CASE STUDY REFLECTIONS

- The teacher, Max, is aware that he needs to deploy the TA as one of his leadership responsibilities.

- He is open to working collaboratively with the TA.

- He does not have the strategies to respond to the TA without feeling confrontational.

- Due to being younger and having less experience in a classroom than the TA he lacks confidence in asserting his authority.

In your feedback to Max, you know that you will need to build his skills and confidence in managing support staff, which can include pragmatic approaches he can draw on to develop his practice. There are several approaches to consider which involves exploring models of working for teachers and TAs, as well as taking a direct approach where all parties engage in a professional dialogue.

MODELS OF TEACHERS AND TAs WORKING TOGETHER

The case study scenario may be an opportunity for you and the mentee to discuss ways that teachers and TAs work together. Vincett et al. (2005) offer three ways of organising the learning environment to facilitate effective teamwork: room management, zoning and reflective teamwork. Each model results in the teacher and TA having clearly defined roles and responsibilities which can be discussed and set out at the beginning of the practice. Through your discussion with Max, you would be able to explore each model, to support him to identify whether one of these models would be effective in his classroom, taking into consideration the children and the relationship he has with the TA.

TRIPARTITE DISCUSSION

One of your skills as a mentor is to problem solve, to deal with potentially difficult situations and to resolve conflict when needed. Through holding a professional discussion, to which all parties can contribute, you can review how the practice is going whilst facilitating dialogue. This intervention is intended to encourage the teacher and TA to share their feelings and thoughts regardless of status. As a facilitator you can support each person to address these, to discuss their reasoning and find a way of working together to benefit the children. An advantage of this problem-solving approach is to highlight the contribution each person can make, whilst identifying a shared aim and a way to work collaboratively on this. It takes time to form an effective team which Tuckman, cited by Bates (2016, p.180), refers to as having four stages: forming, storming, norming and performing. The suggestion is that the ability to work as a team, and find your place within it, takes time and there is a process.

Throughout the support you provide, in a variety of different scenarios, your disposition will be underpinned by, and have taken on board, the school values and ethos. This drives the way that you work and is a framework from which you present the school's expectations and express your viewpoint. From this, mentees will become familiar with your cues about your expectations of them as a teacher as well as developing an understanding about the way things are carried out in the school and why they are done in this way. Whilst recognising the importance of blending in, to feel like a member of the school's staff, it has been acknowledged that teachers new to the profession need to also find their own voice and feel comfortable enough to develop their own character (Cain, 2009). Supporting mentees to juggle these two positions requires you to reflect on your practice, to justify your choices and your professional decisions. This is discussed in relation to your role as a mentor, for you have the ability to have a positive or negative impact upon the development and the competence of the mentee. Your influence is seen through your motivation for being a mentor, which involves taking a look at your perception of yourself. It requires you to step back and ask yourself what your motivation is for being a mentor and whether you understand this role in your school setting.

Perhaps your rationale for being a school mentor includes a mixture of different reasons: maybe it is your desire to develop leadership skills, to share your wide range of experiences or to support a young teacher to develop to their full potential. Your reason for undertaking the role of a school mentor should be driving your work; it provides the starting point and from here you can map out what you are trying to achieve over time.

In the following paragraphs, we will consider the skills and knowledge you use in your role as a school mentor and how you use these in supporting the mentee to uphold high standards of conduct.

KEY REFLECTIONS

- How do you demonstrate high standards in your daily practice, in the classroom and outside school?

- How do you lead by example for all colleagues, parents and the wider school community?

- What training and professional development opportunities do you engage in?

- What coping strategies do you draw on to regain some balance in your professional and personal life?

- How do you look after your health and well-being so that you are confident in looking after others?

PROFESSIONAL RESPONSIBILITIES

Integral to your role are the skills, experience and knowledge that you possess. These are qualities that are unique to you and ones that you bring to the mentoring role. The traditional model of a mentor is one who is highly skilled, very knowledgeable and has the ability to reflect. Through adopting a reflective stance you will be more prepared and more effective in being able to support the development of others (Aspfors and Fransson, 2015). These traits are important to acknowledge and have been highlighted in previous chapters, with efforts to provide an overview of the remit of a school mentor as discussed throughout this book. Now we explore your attributes and responsibilities in the context of Mentor Standard 3: Professionalism. This states how you should:

support the trainee in promoting equality and diversity; ensure the trainee understands and complies with relevant legislation, including that related to the safeguarding of children; and support the trainee to develop skills to manage time effectively. (Teaching Schools Council, 2016, p.12)

The main points are identified and discussed as two key areas: documentation and time management.

DOCUMENTATION

One of your mentoring responsibilities is a commitment to highlight significant legislation and frameworks. Whilst there will be some understanding of curriculum documents, such as Early Years Foundation Stage Framework (DfE, 2017) and the National Curriculum (DfE, 2014), you may need to support your mentee with aspects of practice aligned to delivering the curriculum. It has been stated that school mentors must have excellent subject knowledge and this has been identified as a significant aspect of a mentor's role (Teaching Schools Council, 2016, p.7). Whilst this includes comprehension of a subject, Mutton et al. (2018, p.44) acknowledge this must also include 'specific subject pedagogy'. This not only supports a developing competence in teaching and learning strategies, but also offers the mentee a chance to develop their level of confidence in meeting the Teachers' Standards (DfE, 2011). The ability to convey the reasoning behind *pedagogical* ideas and actions is a skill as you articulate something which is common practice to you but not an everyday act for the colleague you are mentoring (Tsui, 2009). Therefore keeping up to date with your subject knowledge and any curriculum changes is a vital aspect of being a mentor. Not only will you have the opportunity to share your understanding of subject content and structure but, as a mentor, you are also open to learning from the mentee. The relationship you have with your mentee is reciprocal and, needless to say, attributed to your professionalism is the way that you will consider your role as a two-way process with the mentee.

The professional duties of a teacher are shaped by guidance and legislation. Alongside statutory legislation such as curriculum frameworks, the school policies and non-statutory guidance – for example, on school attendance – will all form part of the documentation that will be relevant in the discourse of your relationship with the mentee. Although you will identify which documents are relevant within the context of your school and for the mentee, two clearly identified pieces of legislation have been highlighted in the Mentor Standards (Teaching Schools Council, 2016) and are worth noting at this juncture. These important areas include equality and diversity and safeguarding and these are discussed next. Teachers need to feel confident and familiar with issues relating to these aspects of practice (Carroll and Alexander, 2016).

EQUALITY AND DIVERSITY

Education is a right and should offer all children equal opportunities to learn. Integral to this understanding is that all individuals should be treated the same. In support of promoting equality in the education system, the Equality Act (2010) identifies specific protected characteristics including age, disability, gender, race, religion and belief, and sexual orientation (Hansen, 2015). In response to the Equality Act 2010, schools will have a policy on equality, diversity and inclusion. This will set out the expectations for how the school addresses and eliminates any form of discrimination. Providing a useful starting point, the school policy will be influential towards any discussions on these aspects of practice. Importantly, you may like to consider how you can support inexperienced teachers to identify discrimination and the strategies used to address any concerns. Not only do they need to be aware of the policies on equality and diversity but they also need to feel confident in dealing with any potential issues within these aspects of practice (Carroll and Alexander, 2016). Additionally, as Petty (2009, p.82) states, it is not enough to simply tolerate children based on the group they belong to. They should be treated without bias and be equally valued by staff and within the school. A teacher's responsibility is to consider how equality is promoted in school; your responsibility is to reflect upon how well prepared inexperienced teachers are to deal with potential issues around inequality.

Diversity, set out in the Mentor Standards alongside equality, has gone through a change in the way that the term has been defined. Osler and Solhaug (2018) note the increased concentration upon diversity in education, over the past few decades, in response to population changes. They suggest that, historically, diversity has been aligned to social class. However, more recently, the concepts of language, religion, ethnicity and culture have been added and incorporated into its definition. Additionally, the acts of harassment, discrimination and bullying are also considered to be equality and diversity issues.

Teachers understand that they need to feel confident in their understanding of issues around diversity and how this is central to demonstrating respect for the rights of children. In your role you will be able to provide guidance on how to deal with challenges which includes suggesting appropriate resources or people they can draw upon for specific advice.

SAFEGUARDING

The Mentor Standards ask you to: 'ensure the trainee understands and complies with relevant legislation, including that related to safeguarding of children'

(Teaching Schools Council, 2016, p.12). Legislation includes the statutory and non-statutory guidance and you will be very familiar with this as a member of staff in the school. We focus here on safeguarding as it is a very important aspect of practice in all schools and settings play a significant role in protecting children from abuse. Your role includes letting the mentee know about induction into the role so that they are aware of the school's child protection policies and procedures as well as how they are applied within practice. There will be a staff code of conduct and a school policy on child protection and safeguarding, as well as statutory guidance for schools and colleges on safeguarding children and safer recruitment (DfE, 2018a). There are three key areas that you will be able to consider to structure the support you can provide:

- school ethos

- professional development

- legislation.

To emphasise the supportive ethos of the school, you will be able to draw upon how the welfare and well-being of children is a priority for staff and school governors. What happens in practice to demonstrate this? What advice can you offer which sets out the school's expectations? How is the curriculum organised to allow children to explore potential issues and to learn how to protect themselves from abuse? How is respect and the way staff and children value each other demonstrated, both on a daily basis and as a whole school approach? This includes what teachers do in the classroom, which allows children to feel listened to and which creates a safe place to talk and share concerns in.

Encouraging and advising on appropriate training available is one way to provide support. Keeping on top of the most current practices and training is a key part of your mentor's role to ensure that the best opportunities are utilised. Additionally, the member of staff responsible for child protection and safeguarding – the designated safeguarding lead – in school can offer further support and advice. Other external colleagues such as health practitioners, educational psychology, child and adolescent mental health services, behaviour support, education welfare, social services and specialists in supporting special educational needs may be called upon for support. How can an overview of appropriate external agencies and services be shared with teachers new to the school?

The third aspect, legislation, is used to ensure that everyone is aware of their responsibilities. This clearly includes the school's policies such as the child protection policy, as well as national directives including: *Keeping Children Safe in Education* (DfE, 2018a), which includes information on e-safety; *Working Together* to *Safeguard Children* (DfE, 2018b); and *The Prevent Duty* (DfE, 2015). Are these documents easily accessible and is the system for sharing information within the school clear? The policies cannot be detached from the school's ethos of demonstrating how the adults and children in school show respect for themselves and for each other.

TIME MANAGEMENT

There will never be enough time to do all that has to be done; as one job falls off the list another takes its place. The key to managing this dilemma is to try and find a balance, to learn to prioritise workload and to have an acceptance that you are not superhuman. This is an essential aspect of a teacher's practice that you can help with. Too many teachers are leaving the profession due to workload issues, with around 40 per cent of teachers who begin their initial training not in a state school job five years later (DfE, 2018c). The issues around teacher recruitment and retention are high on the political agenda and this is a key area that policies are addressing. This is an aspect of practice that you need to be aware of so that newly qualified and early career teachers can be encouraged to access support and find enjoyment through being in the teaching profession.

Finding a healthy work–life balance starts with being able to prioritise work and you will be able to advise on how to do this – for example, by starting with a list of tasks, then ranking these jobs into an order of importance. Being well organised and having a clear structure to the tasks that need to be carried out will facilitate effective time management alongside having realistic time frames. Making the most of the resources they have will certainly help in managing their situation. Whilst your support in helping the mentee to manage professional aspects of their practice will be helpful, you may also need to encourage them to reflect upon personal aspects of their life too. At times, personal and professional elements of a teacher's life may need juggling alongside each other to ensure that one is not overloading the other. If teachers can identify stress factors they are more likely to have a positive outlook, and to problem solve and access social-emotional support, which can further enhance their ability to enjoy what they do (Parker and Martin, 2009).

Through your mentoring role you will know when to offer advice, when to make suggestions and when to simply listen without making any judgements. At times it is just enough for the mentee to have your listening ear and a calm stance which can offer them an opportunity to talk about things that may be bothering them. It is helpful if you can support the mentee to develop a positive mindset when dealing with a tricky situation, to help them to work out the choices they have. How can you provide these opportunities when you are also in a demanding role as a mentor? When will you plan in time as well as deal with unexpected situations?

KEY REFLECTIONS

- How is the school ethos upheld by staff and children?

- What are the signs that demonstrate children and staff are treated with respect and dignity?

- What systems are in place to support children and staff to show respect, to feel safe, have a voice and feel listened to?

- How do staff in the school maintain a healthy work–life balance?

PROFESSIONAL RELATIONSHIPS

As a mentor you understand the need to develop a positive and professional relationship with your mentee, as highlighted in Standard 4 of the Mentor Standards – self-development and working in partnership and upholding the expectations of the profession, personally and professionally (Teaching Schools Council, 2016). This includes how you will support the mentee to contribute to the school team and to understand how they fit within the wider school community. There are many ways to do this including encouraging the mentee to start thinking about their interests and skills and identifying a curriculum strength. They could share their expertise with other colleagues or start an after-school club which could be for children or staff.

When working alongside support staff you can help the mentee by informing them about the pedagogical role and responsibilities of support staff. It can help the mentee if they are aware of how this important group of staff can contribute to teaching and learning, including how to involve them in planning and assessment. You could provide helpful advice on how teachers in your school manage their time so that the teacher and TA can discuss planning and assessment. There is a need to support teachers with this aspect of practice if their deployment is to have a positive impact upon pupil progress (Blatchford et al., 2012). Consider the school's work with outside agencies and specialists to help the mentee understand their roles and how they work with the school.

How can you encourage the mentee to share their reflections back in school if they attend an external course or meetings? Is there something that could support the school in its development or further links that could be made with other colleagues?

Working effectively with parents/carers is critical and as you support the mentee discuss aspects of communication including effective ways of responding to a parent/carer's questions and concerns and keeping them informed about their child's progress. It is important that the mentee can deal with unexpected conversations on the playground as well as the more formal scheduled meetings that occur. You have a responsibility to share the school policy on the expectations of working with parents/carers. This aspect of practice is also a requirement of the Teachers' Standards (DfE, 2011). From your experiences over time it will be helpful to provide guidance about the protocols of organising a positive parent consultation meeting, as the mentee may not have previous experience of this. Alongside the formal statutory meeting with parents/carers to discuss a child's progress, you can encourage the mentee to support parents/carers on a less formal basis. This could be through contributing to the many social events organised through the friends, or parent/teacher association. Another important group of school colleagues includes the school governors and the mentee may not have had experience of working with a governing body. They will need to understand what its role is and how governors help with the school's vision and strategic direction to support its educational performance.

Through encouraging the mentee to construct positive working relationships with a range of different groups, you will be helping them to build and expand a wider network of contacts and support them professionally.

KEY REFLECTIONS

In summary, reflect upon how, in your school setting, you can encourage your mentee to:

- co-ordinate a curriculum subject
- start an extra-curricular activity
- deploy support staff effectively
- attend courses and training sessions, then share ideas and reflections
- prepare for parents' evenings

(Continued)

(Continued)

- engage in parent/teacher association activities (school disco, fairs, bingo and other fundraising events)
- get to know the school governors and outside agencies.

CHAPTER SUMMARY

- Professionalism has been explored within an historical context to provide an insight into how the teaching profession has evolved and is viewed in today's society.
- The concepts of training, recruitment and leadership have been influential in supporting a shift towards a modern view of the teaching profession.
- Professionalism has been explored through Mentor Standard 3 which examines how mentors are role models as they lead by example.
- The professional responsibilities of a mentor involve drawing upon skills and knowledge you have developed over many years of practice.
- Mentors understand the value of having a reflective stance and being a lifelong learner.
- Keeping up to date with curriculum changes, government guidance and initiatives is part of a mentor's role.
- At the heart of a mentor's role is the ability to develop positive working relationships with colleagues, children and the wider school community.

SELF-AUDIT QUESTIONS

- What does professionalism look like in your mentor role?
- How can young teachers be supported to stay in the teaching profession?
- What strategies do you have to manage a healthy balance between your personal and professional life?

- How do you keep up to date with your professional development needs?

- What support can you give to new teachers to feel confident in working with parents/carers?

SUGGESTED FURTHER READING

Betlem, E., Clary, D. and Jones, M. (2018) Mentoring the mentors: professional development through a school-university partnership. *Asia-Pacific Journal of Teacher Education*. https://doi.org/10.1080/1359866X.2018.1504280

Cunningham, B. (ed.) (2008) *Exploring Professionalism*. London: Institute of Education, University of London.

Davey, R. (2013) *The Professional Identity of Teacher Educators*. Oxford: Routledge.

Lofthouse, R. and Hall, E. (2014) Developing practices in teachers' professional dialogue in England: using Coaching Dimensions as an epistemic tool. *Professional Development in Education*, 40(5), 758–78.

REFERENCES

Aspfors, J. and Fransson, G. (2015) Research on mentor education for mentors of newly qualified teachers: a qualitative meta-synthesis. *Teacher and Teacher Education*, 48, 75–86.

Bates, B. (2016). *Learning Theories Simplified* (1st edn). London: SAGE.

Blatchford, P., Russell, A. and Webster, R. (2012) *Reassessing the Impact of Teaching Assistants*. London: Routledge.

Bourke, T., Lidstone, J. and Ryan, M. (2015) Schooling teachers: professionalism or disciplinary power? *Educational Philosophy and Theory*, 4(1), 84–100.

Cain, T. (2009) Mentoring trainee teachers: how can mentors use research? *Mentoring and Tutoring: Partnership in Learning*, 17(1), 53–66.

Carroll, J. and Alexander, G.N. (2016) *The Teachers' Standards in Primary Schools: Understanding and Evidencing Effective Practice*. London: SAGE.

Crook, D. (2008). Some historical perspectives on professionalism. In B. Cunningham (ed.), *Exploring Professionalism*. London: Bedford Way Papers.

Davey, R. (2013) *The Professional Identity of Teacher Educators*. Oxford: Routledge.

Department for Education (DfE) (2011) Teachers' standards: guidance for school leaders, school staff and governing bodies. Available at: https://assets.publishing.service.gov.uk/ government/uploads/system/uploads/attachment_data/file/665520/Teachers__Standards.pdf (accessed 18 April 2019).

Department for Education (2014) National Curriculum in England: Framework for Key Stages 1 to 4. London: Crown Copyright.

Department for Education (2015) The Prevent Duty: Departmental advice for schools and childcare providers. London: Crown Copyright.

Department for Education (2017) Early Years Foundation Stage Curriculum. *Setting the standards for learning, development and care for children from birth to five*. London: Crown Copyright.

Department for Education (2018a) *Keeping Children Safe in Education*. London: Crown Copyright.

Department for Education (2018b) *Working Together to Safeguard Children*. London: Crown Copyright.

Department for Education (2018c) *National Statistics: Schools, Pupils and Their Characteristics: January 2018*. London: Crown Copyright.

Department for Education (2019) *Early Career Framework*. Available at https://assets.publishing. service.gov.uk/government/uploads/system/uploads/attachment_data/file/773705/Early- Career_Framework.pdf (accessed 4 April 2019).

Department for Education and Employment (DfEE) (1998) *Teachers: Meeting the Challenge of Change*. Green Paper. London. Available at: https://webarchive.nationalarchives.gov. uk/20070109075515/http://www.teachernet.gov.uk/docbank/index.cfm?id=1424 (accessed 28 April 2019).

Eraut, M. (1994) *Developing Professional Knowledge and Competence*. London: Falmer Press.

Etzioni, A. (1969) *The Semi-Professions and Their Organization: Teachers, Nurses, Social Workers*. New York: Free Press.

Evans, L. (2011) The 'shape' of teacher professionalism in England: professional standards, performance management, professional development and the changes proposed in the 2010 White Paper. *British Educational Research Journal*, 37(5), 851–70.

George, M. (2018) Teachers amongst most trusted professionals in Britain. *Time Educational Supplement*. 20 November. Available at https://www.tes.com/news/teachers-among-most- trusted-professionals-britain (accessed 28 April 2019).

Hansen, A. (2015) *Primary Professional Studies* (3rd edn). London: SAGE.

Heikkinen, H., Wilkinson, J., Aspfors, J. and Bristol, L. (2018) Understanding mentoring of new teachers: communicative and strategic practices in Australia and Finland. *Teaching and Teacher Education*, 71, 1–11.

Howard, C., Burton, M. and Levermore, D. (2019) *Children's Mental Health and Emotional Well- Being in Primary Schools* (2nd edn). Exeter: Learning Matters.

Hudson, P. (2013) Mentoring as professional development: growth for both mentor and mentee. *Professional Development in Education*, 39(5), 771–83.

Kemmis, S., Heikkinen, H., Fransson, G., Aspfors, J. and Edwards-Groves, C. (2014) Mentoring of new teachers as a contested practice: supervision, support and collaborative self-development. *Teaching and Teacher Education*, 43,154–64.

Lofthouse, R. and Hall, E. (2014) Developing practices in teachers' professional dialogue in England: using Coaching Dimensions as an epistemic tool. *Professional Development in Education*, 40(5), 758–78.

Magee, R. (2017) *Standards in ITT Mentoring: There to be Embraced.* British Educational Research Association. Available at https://www.bera.ac.uk/blog/standards-in-itt-mentoring-there-to-be-embraced (accessed 4 August 2019).

Millerson, G. (1964) *The Qualifying Associations.* London: Routledge and Kegan Paul.

Mutton, T., Burn, K., Hagger, H. and Thirlwall, K. (2018) *Teacher Education Partnerships: Policy and Practice.* Series edited by Menter, I. St Albans: Critical.

Osler, A. and Solhaug, T. (2018) Children's human rights and diversity in schools: framing and measuring. *Research in Comparative and International Education*, 13(2), 276–98.

Parker, P.D., and Martin, A.J. (2009) Coping and buoyancy in the work-place: understanding their effects on teachers' work-related well-being and engagement. *Teaching and Teacher Education*, 25, 68–75.

Petty, G. (2009) *Teaching Today.* Cheltenham: Nelson Thornes.

Sachs, J. (2003) *The Activist Teaching Profession.* Buckingham: Open University Press.

Schön, D.A. (1983) *The Reflective Practitioner: How Professionals Think in Action.* London: Maurice Temple Smith.

Teaching Schools Council (2016) *National Standards for School-Based Initial Teacher Training (ITT) Mentors.* Available at https://assets.publishing.service.gov.uk/government/uploads/system/uploads/attachment_data/file/536891/Mentor_standards_report_Final.pdf (accessed 2 May 2019).

Tsui, A. (2009) Distinctive qualities of expert teachers. *Teachers and Teaching: Theory and Practice*, 15(4), 421–39.

Vincett, K., Cremin, H. and Thomas, G. (2005) *Teachers and Teaching Assistants Working Together.* Berkshire: Open University Press.

Watt, N. (2014) Labour plans to license teachers in new move to raise standards. *Guardian*, 11 January. Available from http://www.theguardian.com/politics/2014/jan/11/labour-license-teachers-raise-standards (accessed 28 April 2019).

Whitty, G. (2008) Changing modes of teacher professionalism: traditional, managerial, collaborative and democratic. In B. Cunningham, *Exploring Professionalism.* London: Bedford Way Press.

Wilkins, R. (2013) A road-map to teacher professionalisation in the UK. *Education Today*, 63(1),10–12.

5

STANDARD 4: SELF-DEVELOPMENT AND WORKING IN PARTNERSHIP

CHAPTER OBJECTIVES

By the end of this chapter, you should be aware of how to

- develop good working relationships with colleagues within your Initial Teacher Training partnership (ITT)

- continue to develop your own mentoring practice by accessing appropriate professional development and engaging with robust research

- continue to develop your own subject and pedagogical expertise by accessing appropriate professional development and engaging with robust research

- ensure consistency by working with other mentors and partners to moderate judgements.

MENTOR STANDARDS

This chapter supports the development of the following Mentor Standard (Teaching Schools Council, 2016b, p.10):

Standard 4

Self-development and working in partnership – Continue to develop their own professional knowledge, skills and understanding and invest time in developing a good working relationship within relevant ITT partnerships.

INTRODUCTION

This chapter will outline some of the ways in which you might facilitate your own professional development as a mentor, whilst focusing on how to work with partners and moderate judgements. These aspects will be explored within a context of research-informed practice.

DEVELOPING GOOD WORKING RELATIONSHIPS WITHIN YOUR ITT PARTNERSHIP

As a professional you will be used to liaising with a range of colleagues and partners both within the school community and beyond: the educational psychologist, chair of governors and community police officer all have a part to play in ensuring success. Whatever the situation, if a partnership is effective the impact on yourself and your pupils can be transformative. Conversely, you will be able to recount situations in which a partnership was not successful. When this occurs the damage that follows can also be transformative, causing long-term damage. It is therefore clearly important that all professional colleagues who are involved in the transitioning of trainee teachers into the profession actively work in positive collaboration despite the challenges we all face.

Lillejord and Børte (2016) contemplate the perceived divide between theory and practice whilst Martin et al. (2011) explore the long-term challenges which have occurred when facilitating strong connections between teacher educators and school-based teacher mentors. They highlight the detachment between what is taught in coursework and the learning opportunities with which a novice teacher might be presented during their time within school. Their reflections highlight the importance of 'bridging boundaries' to develop 'hybrid partnership work' (Martin et al., 2011, p.300). So, practically, what can you as a proactive mentor do to bridge these boundaries and ensure that your relationship with your ITT partners is effective? Lillejord and Børte (2016) stress that whatever actions are taken it is vital that they are beneficial for both parties.

Fundamentally, for the ITT partnership to be effective all parties must be mindful of the context in which the other is working. For the colleague who is not school-based, they will visit you and your mentee within your school context, so remember to share with them an overview of the processes and expectations placed on you in your school-based role. It is easy to assume that they have an awareness of the context in which you work and this is not necessarily the case. A simple way of developing an awareness of your partner's working context could be to become a member of a partnership steering committee. The remit of these committees is to ensure the successful development of the partnership by reviewing successes and areas for development and planning accordingly. Often there is not a huge time commitment and you would have a better overview of the structures and processes within the ITT systems. Your own experiences and suggestions of how the partnership might improve are valuable and your partners would 'welcome you with open arms' if you were to offer to work in collaboration. The *Carter Review of Initial Teacher Training* (Crown Copyright, 2015, p.42) emphasises that effective partnerships have a 'shared vision', so becoming a committee member might be a good way of being involved in the development of this vision.

The best partnerships are built on trust. Chapter 2 explores this trusting relationship between you as a mentor and your mentee, but how do you develop trusting relationships with your ITT partner? Sewell et al. (2018) consider the importance of creating time to clarify any queries and I would suggest that planning timely opportunities to communicate with honesty is vital. As busy professionals, it is not always possible to communicate on a face-to-face basis with your partner, but I would recommend that if you need clarification or support you should contact your partner without hesitation. If issues are left to 'drift' they often grow in complexity and a quick telephone conversation can garner a simple solution where an email trail can lose the gist of the issue.

ACCESSiNG APPROPRiATE PROFESSiONAL DEVELOPMENT (PD) TO ENHANCE YOUR MENTORiNG PRACTiCE

In her review of publications relating to teacher professional development, Avalos (2011) considers its complexity and explores its multifaceted nature. She reflects upon the environmental and personal aspects which have an impact, but deliberates that at the heart of these studies is the need to understand the processes whereby teachers change.

Postholm (2018) reflects that there are formal and informal opportunities for professional development. She focuses her attention on the informal interactions within the school context which are part of the day-to-day life of the teacher professional. One of the key features of this specific PD is that it develops over time.

The Department for Education (2016) also consider that for teacher professional development to be effective it should be sustained over time. Furthermore, they highlight that it should: emphasise an improvement in and evaluation of pupil outcomes, be supported by robust evidence and expertise and ought to include collaboration and professional challenge.

The discrepancy in the preparation of teacher mentors is explored by Bower-Phipps et al. (2016). They contemplate that effective teachers are not always innately the most effective mentors. Palazzolo et al. (2019, p.2) consider that 'mentor readiness is developed through formal preparation ... which influences the mentors' technique, knowledge and approach'. Accordingly, it is vitally important that there are openings for mentors to regularly access professional development opportunities despite the challenges of time and funding that abound in our schools. Hobson et al. (2009) bemoan the fact that there is unrealised potential and also occasional harm if mentors are not effectively prepared for their role. Gardiner and Weisling (2018, p.340) ponder that 'new mentors ... experience a steep learning curve that takes an intellectual and emotional toll'. Nevertheless, taking a positive stance it is interesting to note that Smith and Nadelson (2016) surmise that merely hosting a novice teacher within one's classroom can change a mentor's practice. They cite Weasmer and Woods (2003), who report that mentors feel obliged to work hard and show their finest teaching when watched by a novice and become increasingly reflective, leading to improved practice.

AUDITING YOUR CPD NEEDS

To outline, as alluded to earlier in the chapter, it is clear that teacher professional development is a complex process. Therefore, as a committed mentor, how might you start to consider your own CPD? Furthermore, does the culture within your school support you to reflect and improve upon your pedagogy, mentoring knowledge and skills?

Surely, whatever the focus for development, it is important to start with an audit? Your own CPD is no different and I would advise that you start by taking ownership of an honest overview of your mentoring strengths and areas for growth. Ross and Bruce (2007) highlight that self-assessment is an influential strategy for improving achievement and emphasise the importance of a self-assessment tool. A basic starting point for a self-assessment tool, the *National Standards for School-Based Initial Teacher Training (ITT) Mentors* (Teaching Schools Council, 2016b), if discussed with your own mentor/appraiser, might give you a structure around which to form the basis of your own personal, professional development plan. An additional advantage to this collaborative process is that the senior colleague may well have the power to facilitate the capacity to support your future training.

Once you have considered which areas might be your focus for this support, it would be wise to reflect upon whether Postholm's (2018) aforementioned formal or informal development opportunities (or indeed a mixture of the two) might be best suited to your learning needs. Understandably, there will be limitations depending on funding and time; however, it is important that you prioritise your self-development and there is always a solution to a challenge if we think more broadly.

POSSIBLE OPPORTUNITIES FOR PROFESSIONAL DEVELOPMENT

One way of starting on this journey might be to facilitate what Gardiner and Weisling (2018) call 'shadow mentoring'. Within this approach new mentors are encouraged to be observed or to observe a more experienced mentor colleague. This strategy is not intended to develop novice mentors who merely imitate, but offers a problem-solving opportunity where the new mentor can explore appropriate ways of tackling a contextualised situation. Working alongside a trusted other might be an effective way of you gaining confidence within a new area.

Once your confidence has been further enhanced, you might like to consider cultivating what Gardiner and Weisling (2018) suggest are influential collaborative opportunities. These opportunities have the added benefit of enhancing the practice of everyone involved and structured well can have a long-lasting impact. They could take the form of dedicated staff meeting time to discuss mentoring approaches, TeachMeets with 'quickfire' sharing of expertise from speakers, Twitter hashtags # used to develop a bank of mentoring resources or Skype calls, depending on your school context (if you are a geographically wide-reaching Multi Academy Trust (MAT)) and financial capacity.

Garner and Weisling (2018) go on to recommend that we use these partnerships to focus on developing competence around the essential aspects of mentoring such as cultivating positive relationships or nurturing reflection during post-lesson observations. Whatever way you decide to nurture these professional support networks, the key is to plan well and prioritise the time to ensure they take place.

CASE STUDY: AARON

Aaron has six years' experience of teaching in a large urban Primary school and has been chosen to be a mentor by his senior leadership team (SLT). He is committed to his own professional development and that of colleagues and has an empathetic approach to student teachers.

Despite, or perhaps as a direct result of, their confidence in Aaron, he has not been offered any formal professional development by the SLT in preparation for his new mentoring role. The school have appointed a newly qualified teacher (Lily) and Aaron is to be her mentor. Aaron decides to meet Lily during the summer holiday to formally introduce himself and get to know her better. He wants to share some of the key school policies and procedures and review with her the draft Learning Entitlement Plan that has been devised for her.

Aaron is very much looking forward to supporting Lily and feels flattered to have been given this opportunity ahead of his more experienced colleagues who have mentored NQTs before in school. Nevertheless, his preferred way of working is to have a clear understanding of the expectations that have been placed on him. In this instance, as there has been little opportunity for Aaron to prepare or ask questions, he is feeling a little 'out of his depth'.

- How might Aaron ensure that he supports Lily effectively, but also ensure that his own need for professional development is assured?

- Initially, what might be some of the key actions that Aaron can take to increase his own confidence and enable him to begin the year with the basic knowledge he needs to succeed as a strong professional mentor?

Initially, Aaron might contact a member of the SLT to request clarification about what is expected of him and how his role will align with Lily's Learning Entitlement Plan. Once this has been explored, Aaron should audit what his own PD needs are. He might ask his SLT colleague what professional development support he can receive and if it is possible to consider a 'shadow mentor', as there are other experienced mentoring colleagues in school.

It might be pertinent for the SLT to have a ten-minute 'standing item' on the weekly staff meeting agenda linked to the development of mentoring skills. This could support any of the current mentors or might be led by experienced mentor colleagues. This format would support succession planning so that, in the future, colleagues such as Aaron would already have benefited from some easily accessible mentoring support. Indeed, in the future Aaron might well be able to lead a session himself. This time-effective, low-cost but wide-ranging approach could pay dividends with regard to whole school professional development.

Aaron should reflect on some of the successful strategies that he has previously used with students which might be transferable to his role as a mentor to Lily. He could also approach a more experienced mentoring colleague and ask for some informal advice and 'top tips' should it not be possible to facilitate a 'shadow mentor'.

Aaron needs to ensure that he has time to rest and relax over the summer holidays but could easily set up a professional Twitter account. Following feeds such as @CollectivED1 will enable him to start to read more widely about mentoring in an easily accessible and time-effective way.

KEY REFLECTIONS

- It can be useful for a mentor to reflect upon and audit their mentoring strengths and areas for professional development.

- It is vital that colleagues new to mentoring are given relevant and ongoing CPD in order to successfully support their mentee.

- For a mentor to be effective they need to have clarity about the expectations placed on them in this role.

DEVELOPING YOUR OWN SUBJECT AND PEDAGOGIC EXPERTISE

As considered in Chapter 3, it is noticeable that, within the new Ofsted framework (Crown Copyright, 2019), there is a current emphasis on the wider curriculum in Primary schools. This renewed focus brings into question the importance of the strong subject and pedagogic expertise of teachers in general, but specifically the early career teacher mentor. As a professional mentor there is sometimes the perception that you must be an expert in every field. It is not unusual for you to think that in order to support your mentee you have to be the source of all knowledge. Nevertheless, it is of course desirable that you assure a good level of working subject and pedagogic subject knowledge (PSK), despite what Knight (2017) highlights as the problem of how to enable excellent subject knowledge across such a broad range of subjects within the Primary sector.

Knight (2017) argues that collaboration across the wider school community is a way forward. This gives us a clear approach for supporting the PSK of the busy mentor. You will undoubtedly have areas of subject expertise which enable you to confidently support your mentee. The challenge arises when the area of development you are supporting sits within a subject in which you are underconfident. One of the ways in which you and your mentee might both benefit from support from a subject specialist is via the facilitation of a joint observational opportunity. If your mentee has the opportunity to co-plan with a specialist, it would be a powerful CPD opportunity if you and the specialist teacher observed the lesson together. With the specialist taking the lead regarding feedback, you might then reflect upon whether your focus would have been the same and if the post-observational dialogue would have taken the same course.

ENGAGING WITH ROBUST EDUCATIONAL RESEARCH

WHY STRIVE TO BE RESEARCH-INFORMED?

The *Carter Review of Initial Teacher Training* (Crown Copyright, 2015, p.27) considers that, 'high performing systems induct their teachers in the use, assessment and application of research findings and that schools should be research-rich environments'. Flynn (2019) suggests that there has been a fascination for years, from policy-makers and researchers, in the conviction that teachers should seek to improve through engagement with research. She surmises that one of the challenges is the lack of clarity around what 'evidence-informed' or 'research-engaged' actually means. In addition, she feels that there is tension between hard-working teachers who have an everyday focus on their students and busy researchers, discovering ways of making their findings readily available.

Brown and Zhang (2016) ask us to contemplate that 'evidence' can come from practitioners or researchers and that both are equally valid. Additionally, they ask that practitioners use their research to enhance practice, rather than reusing research that has been reported elsewhere. Godfrey (2017, p.442) develops this celebration of practitioner research and explores the notion of joint practice development, praising the National College of Teaching and Leadership report on evidence-based teaching (Hammersley-Fletcher et al., 2015) for its 'more nuanced understanding of the relationship between teaching and research evidence'. This report promotes the structures of lesson study, research cafés, TeachMeets and journal clubs. They are considered pertinent ways to access evidence which can inform professional practice. I concur that the busy mentor may find that these approaches can be easily embedded into everyday school life as they are inexpensive in terms of financial cost and also time.

As depicted in Figure 5.1 over the page, in their case study of United Learning schools, Judkins et al. (2014) found that professionals engaging with research believed it enhanced one's ability to reflect more deeply. You can see from the image that research evidence enabled colleagues to gain a wider perspective and become more confident. Moreover, teacher professionals were perceived to have an open-minded approach to developing different pedagogical practices. It is clear to see that open-mindedness was considered by teachers and senior leaders to permeate the whole school community, creating a cycle of enquiry and innovation.

The opportunity to develop increased depth of reflection and a more holistic viewpoint is a vital tool in your repertoire of support and, as mentioned above, there are a range of ways in which you can exploit research to strengthen your day-to-day work.

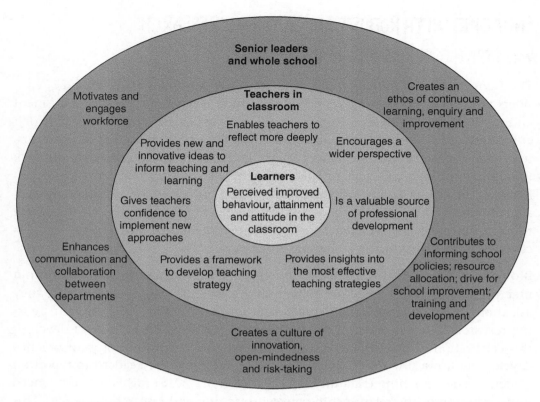

Figure 5.1   Perceived benefits of engagement in research evidence Judkins et al. (2014, p.4)

Nevertheless, the Teaching Schools Council (2016a, pp.16–17) warn against a 'scattergun approach' and caution that it is vital for you to gauge whether research is high quality and has been well evidenced. Specifically, they request that we consider: consistency of findings, any conflict of interests, the research credibility and any contrasting evidence. So, where might you seek out such informed resources?

Recent years have seen the expansion of easily accessible and inexpensive research resources online and, as mentioned in Chapter 3, the Chartered College of Teaching have one such portal (https://chartered.college) which abounds with 'easy to read' and accessible research. Members are entitled to a hard copy of a termly, peer-reviewed journal and if you are a mentor who prefers not to read on screen, you can develop a bank of relevant resources for an inexpensive membership fee.

Another source of credible research has been collated and developed by Professor Rachel Lofthouse, Professor of Teacher Education in the Carnegie School of Education. The Research and Practice Centre 'CollectivED: The Mentoring and Coaching Hub' (www.leedsbeckett.ac.uk/carnegie-school-of-education/research/

working-paper-series/collectived) enables access to working papers developed by a wide range of practitioners who have submitted articles. The aim of this hub is to encourage 'scholarship and debate' (Leeds Beckett University Carnegie School of Education, various dates) and I recommend that you to consider the papers to find discussion points for you and your mentee to debate or the wider school community to reflect upon.

CASE STUDY: JACK

Jack has taught for six years in a one-form entry junior school. Two years ago he became a mentor to Elly, a novice teacher. Elly passed her induction year with Jack's support and there were aspects of Jack's mentoring approach that he, and his SLT, felt enabled Elly to confidently develop her practice. Jack manages his time effectively and also has excellent subject knowledge. He shared some of his strategies for managing a work–life balance with Elly and helped her develop her own subject knowledge in Mathematics. This year Jack's senior leadership team have asked Jack to mentor a newly qualified teacher, Arjun. Jack is looking forward to supporting Arjun but knows, after talking to an SLT colleague during his own annual appraisal, that one area he needs to develop is his own use of research. He is unsure what research-informed teaching might look like in the classroom or how to develop it. How might Jack, further develop his own research-informed practice so that he can better help Arjun to develop his pedagogical approach?

Initially, Jack might ask his appraiser for clarity about what the school's definition is of 'research-informed teaching'. He could explore whether this will be a focus for the whole school or a select group of colleagues and what PD support will be available, including opportunities to engage with wider school research.

Next, Jack might read the National College of Teaching and Leadership report on evidence-based teaching (Hammersley-Fletcher et al., 2015) to give himself a greater overview of what being research-informed might mean for him. He and Arjun could become members of the Chartered College and explore one of the research articles from the journals each time they meet. Jack might also log onto www.eventbrite.co.uk to see if there are any TeachMeets planned in his local area that they, and other school colleagues, could attend.

> ## KEY REFLECTIONS
>
> - Engaging in research and being research-informed can have wide-ranging positive effects for a whole school community.
>
> - It is important for you as a mentor to ensure that the research you consider is credible.
>
> - There are a wide range of easily accessible, research-informed resources that you as a busy mentor can access and share with your mentee.

CONSISTENCY OF PRACTICE

Whatever the route into teaching the trainee takes, all colleagues who are awarded Qualified Teacher Status (QTS) are expected to be adequately prepared for the rigors of the profession. Whether this involves ensuring an excellent understanding of strategies for managing challenging behaviour, a confident knowledge of the pedagogy within specific areas such as phonics or an effective understanding of how to assess calculation skills, the novice teacher's role is multifaceted and ensuring an accurate judgement of their aptitude is a challenge. It is a statutory expectation that, 'Trainee assessment procedures should be rigorous and robust, supporting consistent and accurate judgements' (DfE, 2019a, C2.1). Whatever the preferred route, these judgements are made in collaboration between professional partners and it is vital that the procedures used enable a reliable assessment of their teaching capabilities.

Similarly, within the induction year, an appropriate body should be utilised to quality assure that 'assessment is fair and consistent across all institutions' (DfE, 2018, p.13). Again, this reinforces the national expectation that all NQTs are assessed in a way that ensures consistent assessment to prevail. With such clearly expressed national expectations, we expect that it must be a relatively simple task to ensure a consistent approach. How disingenuous a notion this is.

Spooner-Lane (2017) cites a lack of resourcing and funding which stops schools evaluating their mentoring programmes. She surmises this leads to increased variation in the implementation and conceptualisation of mentoring. I concur, but would emphasise that many school mentors give early career teachers excellent support. Undoubtably, however, for the novice there is no guarantee that in whichever school they complete their induction year they will benefit from dedicated mentoring and guidance. In their *Teacher Recruitment and Retention Strategy*

(DfE, 2019b), the government pledges to fully fund training for mentors and proposes funding for dedicated mentoring time. These proposals are a welcome development, but this pledge must come to fruition if our profession is to recruit the best potential teachers and retain our most effective colleagues.

Contemplating the importance of the mentor to pre-service teachers, Hudson (2016) highlights wide variations in mentor practice with regard to aspects of constructive professional feedback. He considers that lesson observations are problematic as mentors have an array of foci to consider effectively. As educators we know the complexity of the classroom learning environment; therefore, agreeing an area of observational focus with your mentee beforehand is a wise decision which can lead to a more consistent approach. Lofthouse and Wright (2012, p.95) ask us to consider a practitioner enquiry observation tool which reduces the multitude of foci for the observer.

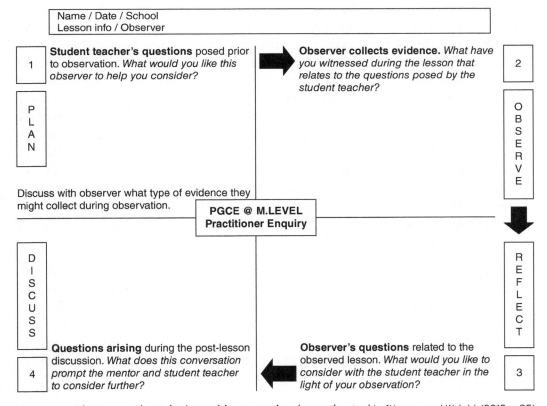

Figure 5.2 *The revised practitioner enquiry observation tool* Lofthouse and Wright (2012, p.95)

As clearly defined in Figure 5.2, questions generated by the novice observee become the starting point for the enquiry, with the mentor focusing on the recording of 'evidence' observed rather than making a judgement based on their own expectations and cultural values. Empowering for the early career teacher, Lofthouse and Wright (2012) surmise that this process also provokes the mentor to consider more closely their role within the feedback relationship. This observation tool might therefore be a useful starting point for you and your partners to promote reflection (as evident in the figure on the previous page) and ownership for everyone involved. Moreover, utilised by other colleagues across the school it could be a source of rich, dialogic consideration in staff meetings and a powerful professional development tool with staff ownership at the core.

Variable interpretations of criteria, such as those used within observations, are also contemplated by Zsargo and Palmer (2019), who believe that this lack of consistency creates tension for mentors. They expand by stating that the dichotomous role of the mentor and the contexts in which they operate, in addition to their own personal constructs, place on them an 'ethical burden' in their search for consistency. They bemoan a subjective system which is constructed within a range of complex influences. Indeed, we know that all lessons and observations are unique depending on: the age, heritage and supposed ability of the pupils; the curricular subject considered, the time of day, week, year before we even try to consider the built environment of the classroom; the adults involved in the learning; and the lens through which the observer observes. So, how do they believe some form of consistency be attained? Zsargo and Palmer (2019) suggest that routine and meaningful formative discussions between mentors and trainees (and tutors) which explore the strengths and development areas of pedagogy are a key strategy. I would counter, however, that these conversations are only meaningful if all parties have an equal voice and can confidently, yet empathetically speak their mind. Izadinia (2016) emphasises the importance of open communication and a non-judgemental approach and asks us to value the influence of our role in shaping our mentee's future professional identity.

Hudson (2016) studies Tillema (2009), who argues that this range of perceptions can be positive for your mentee. He states that this variation may enhance the nature of information given and, like Tillema, considers the development of a community of mentors to be a supportive concept. Like Hudson (2016), Holland (2018, p.119) considers the power of mentoring communities of practice and he details the impact of this approach as providing opportunities for 'Knowledge expansion' and the ability for mentors to 'reframe thinking'.

Simplistically, access to a community of mentors can be facilitated either internally within your organisation or externally beyond the school. Depending on the size of the institution in which you work: large MAT, small, rural Primary school, large urban teaching school, I would suggest that developing processes whereby you are able to have regular, constructive mentoring conversations with other colleagues within your school or beyond would be a positive step to take in the search for consistency. For example, these conversations might consider some of the pedagogic challenges that the novice faces and may well support a critical consideration of strategic steps to be taken to enable the best outcome for all. Similarly, expectations of teaching aptitude might be discussed so that all colleagues gauge the ability of the novice at the stage at which they are learning, rather than as an experienced other. Additionally, I would argue that your role as a mentor is multifaceted and complex, so this symbiotic approach would support your well-being, ensuring that you do not feel pressured into managing the time-consuming and intense relationship with your novice mentee in isolation. It is challenging to remain positive and also have a neutral stance when an intense professional relationship begins to invade 'the day job'!

PARTNERSHIPS BEYOND SCHOOL

Beyond the school gates, wider partnerships can be effective in the search for consistency. Within the growing complexity and fragmented landscape of the national structure of initial teacher education, Lofthouse (2018) explores the vulnerability of these partnerships. She argues that the quality of mentoring becomes increasingly significant within this disjointed context. So, how can you as a mentor secure partnership support which enables you to develop a consistent approach? Betlem et al. (2019, p.340) explore the mutually beneficial partnership of teacher mentors and academic partners and call for greater opportunities to become 'practiced in collaboration'. On the whole, universities that facilitate teacher training courses offer opportunities for mentor training on a regular basis within their partnership. Frequently, however, it is the case that despite being offered financial assistance some teacher mentors might not attend due to significant in-school pressures. One way that university colleagues have navigated these hurdles is by using a blended learning approach. Fransson (2016) suggests that although e-learning is no substitute for face-to-face communication, there is a benefit of accessibility that the busy mentor would find valuable. Mentor training that is delivered online is increasingly becoming a way in which busy colleagues can collaborate. With the multitude of communication platforms and APPs now available such as 'Skype for business' and 'Collaborate', I would suggest that if you are unable to access face-to-face PD you might urge your partners to consider an e-learning approach. Alternatively, if feeling proactive, you might develop your own online community of practice in order to enhance your personal development and that of your mentee.

CHAPTER SUMMARY

It is vital that mentors work collaboratively with partners, either via face-to-face opportunities or online, to moderate judgements and ensure consistent approaches.

- Timely communication is vital if partnerships are to flourish.

- A community of mentors can be a powerful way for colleagues to access support and remove feelings of isolation.

- All mentors have an entitlement to regular professional development opportunities if they are to perform their role effectively.

- There are many ways for a mentor to access professional development opportunities. These may include more formal methods such as conferences and staff meetings or informal opportunities such as peer discussion.

- There are many ways in which a mentor can become 'research-informed' such as joining a research journal club or attending a TeachMeet.

SELF-AUDIT QUESTIONS

- How might you ensure that your mentoring judgements and working routines align with best practice?

- How might you further develop your research knowledge? What resources could you seek out and who might you share this knowledge with?

SUGGESTED FURTHER READING

Shanks, R. (2017) Mentoring beginning teachers: professional learning for mentees and mentors. *International Journal of Mentoring and Coaching in Education*, 6(3), 158–63.

Marciano, J.E., Farver, S.D., Guenther, A., Wexler, L.J., Jansen, K. and Stanulis, R.N. (2019) Reflections from the room where it happens: examining mentoring in the moment. *International Journal of Mentoring and Coaching in Education*, 8(2), 134–48.

REFERENCES

Avalos, B. (2011) Teacher professional development in teaching and teacher education over ten years. *Teaching and Teacher Education*, 27(1), 10–20. Available at https://www.sciencedirect.com/science/article/pii/S0742051X10001435 (accessed 23 July 2019).

Betlem, E., Clary, D. and Jones, M. (2019) Mentoring the mentor: professional development through a school–university partnership. *Asia-Pacific Journal of Teacher Education*, 47(4), 327–46. Available at doi: 10.1080/1359866X.2018.1504280 (accessed 21 July 2019).

Bower-Phipps, L., Van Senus Klecka, C. and Sature A.L. (2016) Developing mentors: an analysis of shared mentoring practices. *The New Educator*, 12(3), 289–308. Available at doi: 10.1080/1547688X.2016.1187979 (accessed 21 July 2019).

Brown, C. and Zhang, D. (2016) Is engaging in evidence-informed practice in education rational? What accounts for discrepancies in teachers' attitudes towards evidence use and actual instances of evidence use in schools? *British Educational Research Journal*, 42(5), 780–801.

Crown Copyright (2015) *Carter Review of Initial Teacher Training (ITT)*. Available at https://assets.publishing.service.gov.uk/government/uploads/system/uploads/attachment_data/file/399957/Carter_Review.pdf (accessed 14 August 2019).

Crown Copyright (2019) *The Education Inspection Framework*. Available at 'https://assets.publishing.service.gov.uk/government/uploads/system/uploads/attachment_data/file/801429/Education_inspection_framework.pdf (accessed 12 August 2019).

Department for Education (DfE) (2016) Standard for teachers' professional development. Available at https://assets.publishing.service.gov.uk/government/uploads/system/uploads/attachment_data/file/537030/160712_-_PD_standard.pdf (accessed 23 July 2019).

Department for Education (2018) Induction for newly qualified teachers (England) Statutory guidance for appropriate bodies, headteachers, school staff and governing bodies. Available at https://assets.publishing.service.gov.uk/government/uploads/system/uploads/attachment_data/file/696428/Statutory_Induction_Guidance_2018.pdf (accessed 21 July 2019).

Department for Education (2019a) *Initial Teacher Training (ITT): Criteria and Supporting Advice*. Available at https://www.gov.uk/government/publications/initial-teacher-training-criteria/initial-teacher-training-itt-criteria-and-supporting-advice#management-and-quality-assurance-criteria (accessed 21 July 2019).

Department for Education (2019b) *Teacher Recruitment and Retention Strategy*. Available at https://www.gov.uk/government/publications/teacher-recruitment-and-retention-strategy (accessed 12 August 2019).

Flynn, N. (2019) Facilitating evidence-informed practice. *Teacher Development*, 23(1), 64–82. Available at doi10.1080/13664530.2018.1505649 (accessed 23 July 2019).

Fransson, G. (2016) Online (web-based) education for mentors of newly qualified teachers. *International Journal of Mentoring and Coaching in Education*, 5(2), 111–26.

Gardiner, W. and Weisling, N. (2018) Challenges and complexities of developing mentors' practice: insights from new mentors. *International Journal of Mentoring and Coaching in Education*, 7(4), 329–42. Available at doi 10.1108/IJMCE-12-2017-0078 (accessed 21 July 2019).

Godfrey, D. (2017) What is the proposed role of research evidence in England's 'self-improving' school system? *Oxford Review of Education*, 43(4), 433–46.

Hammersley-Fletcher, L., Lewin, C., with Davies, C., Duggan, J., Rowley, H. and Spink, E. (2015) Evidence based teaching: advancing capability and capacity for enquiry in schools: Interim report. Available at https://assets.publishing.service.gov.uk/government/uploads/system/uploads/attachment_data/file/464596/EBT_Interim_report_FINAL.pdf (accessed 23 July 2019).

Hobson, A.J., Ashby, P., Malderez, A. and Tomlinson, P.D. (2009) Mentoring beginning teachers: what we know and what we don't. *Teaching and Teacher Education*, 25(1), 207–16.

Holland, E. (2018) Mentoring communities of practice: what's in it for the mentor? *International Journal of Mentoring and Coaching in Education*, 7(2), 110–26. Available at doi/10.1108/IJMCE-04-2017-0034/full/html (accessed 21 July 2019).

Hudson, P. (2016) Identifying mentors' observations for providing feedback. *Teachers and Teaching*, 22(2), 219–34. Available at doi: 10.1080/13540602.2015.1055446 (accessed 21 July 2019).

Izadinia, M. (2016) Student teachers' and mentor teachers' perceptions and expectations of a mentoring relationship: do they match or clash? *Professional Development in Education*, 42(3), 387–402.

Judkins, M., Stacey, O., McCrone, T. and Inniss, M. (2014) Teachers' use of research evidence a case study of United Learning schools. Available at https://www.nfer.ac.uk/publications/IMUL01/IMUL01.pdf (accessed 22 July 2019).

Knight, R. (2017) The subject and the setting: re-imagining opportunities for primary teachers' subject knowledge development on school-based teacher education courses. *Teachers and Teaching*, 23(7), 843–58.

Leeds Beckett University Carnegie School of Education (various dates) CollectiveEd working paper series. Available at https://www.leedsbeckett.ac.uk/carnegie-school-of-education/research/working-paper-series/collectived/ (accessed 22 July 2019).

Lillejord, S. and Børte, K. (2016) Partnership in teacher education: a research mapping. *European Journal of Teacher Education*, 39(5), 550–63. Available at doi 10.1080/02619768.2016.1252911 (accessed 14 August 2019).

Lofthouse, R.M. (2018) Re-imagining mentoring as a dynamic hub in the transformation of initial teacher education: the role of mentors and teacher educators. *International Journal of Mentoring and Coaching in Education*. Available at https://www.emerald.com/insight/content/doi/10.1108/IJMCE-04-2017-0033/full/html (accessed 18 July 2019).

Lofthouse, R. and Wright, D. (2012) Teacher education lesson observation as boundary crossing. *International Journal of Mentoring and Coaching in Education*, 1(2), 89–103.

Martin, S.D., Snow, J.L. and Franklin Torrez, C.A. (2011) Navigating the terrain of third space: tensions with/in relationships in school–university partnerships. *Journal of Teacher Education*, 62(3), 299–311. Available at doi: 10.1177/0022487110396096 (accessed 14 August 2019).

Palazollo, A., Shahbazi, S. and Salinitri, G. (2019) Working towards change: the impact of mentor development on associate teachers and faculty advisors. *Interchange 0826-4805*. Available at doi:10.1007/s10780-019-09365-1 (accessed 21 July 2019).

Postholm, M.B. (2018) Teachers' professional development in school: a review study. *Cogent Education*, 5(1). Available at https://search.proquest.com/docview/2176649053?pq-origsite=summon&accountid=15133 (accessed 23 July 2019).

Ross, J.A. and Bruce, C.D. (2007) Teacher self-assessment: a mechanism for facilitating professional growth. *Teaching and Teacher Education*, 23(2), 146–59.

Sewell, A., Cody, T., Weir, K. and Hansen, S. (2018) Innovations at the boundary: an exploratory case study of a New Zealand school–university partnership in initial teacher education. *Asia-Pacific Journal of Teacher Education*, 46(4), 321–39. Available at doi/pdf/10.1080/13598 66X.2017.1402294 (accessed 14 August 2019).

Smith, J. and Nadelson, L. (2016) Learning for you and learning for me: mentoring as professional development for mentor teachers. *Mentoring and Tutoring: Partnership in Learning*, 24(1), 59–72. Available at doi: 10.1080/13611267.2016.1165489 (accessed 23 July 2019).

Spooner-Lane, R. (2017) Mentoring beginning teachers in Primary schools: research review. *Professional Development in Education*, 43(2), 253–73. Available at doi: 10.1080/19415 257.2016.1148624 (accessed 21 July 2019).

Teaching Schools Council (2016a) *Effective Primary Teaching Practice*. Available at https://tactyc.org.uk/wp-content/uploads/2016/08/Effective-primary-teaching-practice-2016-report-web.pdf (accessed 22 July 2019).

Teaching Schools Council (2016b) *National Standards for School-Based Initial Teacher Training (ITT) Mentors*. Available at https://assets.publishing.service.gov.uk/government/uploads/system/uploads/attachment_data/file/536891/Mentor_standards_report_Final.pdf (accessed 23 July 2019).

Tillema, H.H. (2009) Assessment for learning to teach: appraisal of practice teaching lessons by mentors, supervisors, and student teachers. *Journal of Teacher Education*, 60(2), 155–67.

Weasmer, J. and Woods, A.M. (2003) Mentoring: professional development through reflection'.*The Teacher Educator*, 39, 65–77. Available at https://www.researchgate.net/publication/233073685_Mentoring_Professional_development_through_reflection (accessed 23 July 2019).

Zsargo, E. and Palmer, J. (2019) Common understanding or 'hodgepodge'? The consistency and accuracy of school-based mentors' assessment of trainee primary teachers in England. *Teacher Education Advancement Network Journal*. Available at https://pure.hud.ac.uk/ws/portalfiles/portal/16117344/Zsargo_Palmer_paper_TEAN_journal_submission.pdf (accessed 22 July 2019).

6

PROFESSIONAL MENTORING SKILLS

CHAPTER OBJECTIVES

By the end of this chapter you should be aware of:

- ways in which your self-awareness, including an understanding of your values and beliefs, can inform your mentoring practice
- how contracting can support the development of an effective mentoring relationship
- a range of skills required for effective mentoring
- how your mentoring skills can aid your mentee's thinking and learning.

MENTOR STANDARDS

This chapter supports the development of the following Mentor Standards (Teaching Schools Council, 2016, p.10):

- Standard 1 – Personal qualities: Establish trusting relationships, modelling high standards of practice, and empathising with the challenges a trainee faces.
- Standard 2 – Teaching: Support trainees to develop their teaching practice in order to set high expectations and to meet the needs of all pupils.
- Standard 3 – Professionalism: Induct the trainee into professional norms and values, helping them to understand the importance of the role and responsibilities of teachers in society.

- Standard 4 – Self-development and working in partnership: Continue to develop their own professional knowledge, skills and understanding and invest time in developing a good working relationship within relevant ITT partnerships.

INTRODUCTION

This chapter will focus upon professional mentoring skills that will enable mentors to provide effective support and challenge to their mentees. It establishes the importance of being aware of our own values and beliefs, as these will influence the way in which we provide mentoring support, and then explores specific skills and ways in which a mentor can develop them further. It identifies and discusses skills that can help you as a mentor to grow 'the individual, both professionally and personally' (DfE, 2018, p.27), both during their training and through the early stages of their career.

WHAT ARE PROFESSIONAL MENTORING SKILLS?

As a mentor, you will have a significant impact on your mentees, on your partnership institution and, professionally, on yourself. Government publications on mentoring usually state that a mentor should be an experienced teacher and suitable role model, but most do not specify many of the skills required for effective mentoring. One exception is the government's response to the consultation on strengthening qualified teacher status which states that:

> *mentor training should include the development of specific, focused skills such as providing effective feedback, facilitating supportive conversations and holding challenging conversations to ensure the mentoring is high-quality rather than generic.* (DfE, 2018, p.18)

Every mentor will have different skills, and to varying levels, when they take on a mentoring role – for example, some will be better at listening, or at asking questions, than others. Whatever your skill level, this chapter will help you to reflect upon your mentoring skills and find ways to develop them even further.

As mentioned in Chapter 1, it is difficult to provide an exact and agreed definition of mentoring. Many people have also sought to clarify the difference between mentoring and coaching. Helpfully, Clutterbuck (2018) has stressed the commonality rather than the differences:

*The non-directive, questioning style is common to both coaching and mentoring –
not surprising really, when coaching derives from mentoring … The differentiation is
that mentors bring relevant experience and provide context (information or perspectives the learner doesn't have) to help the learner better understand their internal
and external world, so they can make better decisions … John Leary-Joyce described
mentoring … as coaching plus – the plus being domain insight and the wisdom to
use it sparingly.* (Clutterbuck, 2018)

As can be seen from Downey's spectrum of coaching skills (2014, p.18) shown at
Figure 6.1, the closer a mentor is to the directive end of the spectrum the greater
ownership of the conversation they are taking as they are telling their mentee
what to do. When the mentor is closer to the non-directive end of the spectrum,
the mentor is listening and playing their mentee's words and ideas back to
them thereby giving the mentee greater ownership of the discussion. The mentor is therefore encouraging the mentee to identify their own options and reach
their own decisions about the way forward. Effective mentors will balance these
directive and non-directive approaches to most effectively aid their mentee's development and their ability to make informed decisions.

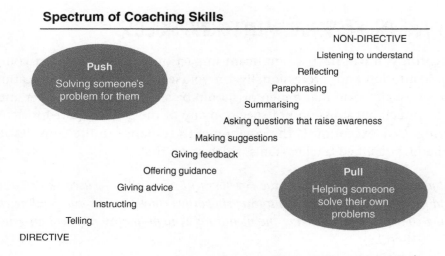

Spectrum of Coaching Skills

NON-DIRECTIVE
Listening to understand
Push
Reflecting
Solving someone's
problem for them
Paraphrasing
Summarising
Asking questions that raise awareness
Making suggestions
Giving feedback
Offering guidance
Pull
Giving advice
Helping someone
solve their own
problems
Instructing
Telling
DIRECTIVE

Figure 6.1   Spectrum of coaching skills (Downey, 2014)

An effective mentor tailors their approach to each mentee's needs. For example, a
mentee who is training to be a teacher may benefit from a more directive approach
(at least initially) whilst those who have completed their training and are in the
early years of their teaching career may benefit from a non-directive approach as
they will have experiences to draw upon.

Each approach will be useful during a mentee's journey – the art of effective mentoring is to judge what the most appropriate approach is, at any particular time, to maximise the mentee's learning and development.

CASE STUDY: SAMIRA

When reflecting upon her experiences of being mentored whilst training to be a primary school teacher, Samira said: 'feedback from lesson observations would be non-directive, with my mentor asking a series of open questions such as "How did you think that went?" Only after I'd expressed my views would he give me his feedback and advice. His non-directive approach made me feel valued as a professional as he listened to my opinions and I could openly reflect on my own practice. It helped to build my confidence as I felt that I was being respected and that I could teach. I had a lot to learn, but he encouraged me to reflect upon my actions and approaches.'

CASE STUDY REFLECTIONS

As can be seen from Samira's comments, her mentor did not jump in with his own feedback and ideas following a lesson observation – instead, he asked Samira to critique her own performance. By doing so, he was encouraging her to reflect and to take responsibility for assessing what she had done. The impact of this approach was that Samira felt valued and respected, it helped to build her confidence, and it will also have ensured that she did not rely on her mentor. By asking Samira to assess her own performance, her mentor was ensuring that she reflected upon her own practice and played an active role in the mentoring discussion.

This chapter focuses upon some of the skills that are closer to the non-directive end of the spectrum as we have assumed that more directive skills – such as 'telling', 'instructing' and 'giving advice' – will already be well developed in most teachers as they are skills that are regularly used within the classroom. The skills covered within this chapter are therefore:

- contracting

- building rapport

- active listening

- questioning

- summarising

- challenging

- giving feedback.

Before starting to explore these skills, it is important to consider your values and beliefs as, whoever you are mentoring and whatever their situation, your values and beliefs will influence your mentoring approach; what you consider to be important, and what you hold to be true, will affect your responses to what others say and do.

VALUES AND BELIEFS

The online Oxford Dictionary (2019) provides the following definitions for values and beliefs:

- Values: *'Principles or standards of behaviour; one's judgement of what is important in life'*.

- Beliefs: *'Something one accepts as true or real; a firmly held opinion'*.

Values are ideals we hold that give significance and meaning to our own lives and they therefore underpin our beliefs (Pask and Joy, 2007). As values are subjective, what one person regards as important may not be considered important by another person.

Munro Turner (2004) recommends that, before we seek to understand others' values and beliefs, we must first be aware of our own values and beliefs. He suggests that our values influence what we 'notice, think, feel, choose and do' (p. 4) and has suggested some questions that can help to identify someone else's values:

- *'What interests you?'* (to identify perceptions and thoughts)

- *'What do you enjoy?'* (to identify feelings)

- *'What is important to you?'* (to identify choices made)

- *'What do you spend your time doing?'* (to identify actions taken).

Another way of exploring values is to complete the (free at the time of writing) online VIA Character Strengths survey (available at https://www.viacharacter.org/www/Character-Strengths-Survey) and to receive your personal VIA report. This

VIA report, as the name implies, will focus upon your 'strengths', described as 'the positive parts of your personality that impact how you think, feel and behave' (VIA Institute on Character, 2019).

When you are starting to work with a new mentee, you could both complete the VIA Characters Strengths survey – or a different exercise/survey linked to values – and then compare and discuss your individual responses. Look for areas of similarity and areas of difference, and explore how some of those at the top and the bottom of the scale have been evidenced in your approach to teaching. This will help you to get to know each other and start to build a relationship. Within your mentoring conversations, you could also ask questions that will help you to identify some of your mentee's values.

It is also worth noting that each organisation has its own values which, in turn, inform the organisational culture. The match (or mismatch) between our own values and those of the organisation we work for can lead to our contentment within, or our conflict with, that workplace.

Whilst our values relate to things that are important to us, our beliefs are ideas that we no longer question (Thomas and Smith, 2009). Our beliefs are generalisations we have created about the way things should be done and they therefore influence our judgements of ourselves and others ... yet our beliefs are often wrong (Argyris, 1990).

As well as being aware of your own beliefs, you will gain an insight into your mentee's beliefs through mentoring and can try to counter any 'limiting beliefs' that are holding them back. 'Limiting beliefs', and ways in which you can help your mentees to recognise and address them, are considered in Chapter 7.

KEY REFLECTIONS

- What are your values and beliefs?

- Can you think of a situation where your values or beliefs have affected your reaction to someone you were working with?

- If you have completed the VIA Character Strengths survey mentioned above, focus upon your top three character strengths and consider how they have informed, or might inform, your approach to mentoring.

CONTRACTING

Before focusing on some of the skills required for mentoring, we need to consider the foundations for a mentoring relationship to ensure that all parties are clear about what is involved. Without this foundation, a mentoring relationship is more likely to founder.

Contracting is an ethical method of framing expectations and responsibilities before the mentoring relationship commences. Clutterbuck (2014) does not necessarily advocate the use of a formal contract, but does recommend that a discussion take place between you and your mentee about the ways in which you will be working with each other. This relationship could also be evaluated, at various stages, by referring back to your contracting discussion (or contracting document, if you created one).

Your contracting discussion could include a two-way exchange about:

- Objectives: What are we hoping to achieve through this mentoring relationship?

- Expectations: What can the mentor expect of the mentee and vice versa?

- Responsibilities: Who will do what and when?

- Confidentiality: What information will be passed on to others, under what circumstances, and what will remain between mentor and mentee?

Parsloe and Leedham (2016) regard contracting as a means of helping a mentee to accept responsibility for the process – this is linked to Connor and Pokora's (2012) view that mentees should be encouraged to take charge of their own development.

KEY REFLECTIONS

- What contracting took place during your last mentoring relationship?

- How did this contracting (or lack of it) impact upon the effectiveness of the mentoring relationship?

- What might you do differently in future?

BUILDING RAPPORT

Rapport is defined by the online Oxford Dictionary (2019) as 'A close and harmonious relationship in which the people or groups concerned understand each other's feelings or ideas and communicate well'. It is important to consider how you can maximise the chances of developing a positive relationship with your mentee as there is often a link between the quality of the mentoring relationship and the mentee's outcomes (Lenz, 2014).

Corradi (1990) believes that relationships are natural and either happen or not, whilst Thomas and Smith (2009) consider the basic ingredients to include chemistry, mutual trust, respect and freedom of expression. However, Flaherty (2010) suggests that a positive mentoring relationship is built on openness, fairness and commitment rather than on chemistry.

Tolhurst (2010) argues that rapport building is a skill that can be learned, and Lancer et al. (2016) take the view that rapport is developed over a number of sessions. You can build rapport with your mentee by:

- demonstrating genuine interest: asking what is important to them/eliciting their values: *'What are you passionate about?'; 'What would you like your pupils to think about/say about you?'*

- establishing trust: doing what you say you will do (which links back to 'contracting') and behaving in an ethical manner. As a mentor you are playing a key role in an early career teacher's development and they need to trust you to make accurate and fair judgements on their practice

- openness: being willing to share your thoughts and feelings

- empathy: imagining what it might be like to be in the mentee's situation and what they might be feeling

- body language: including eye contact, facial expressions, an open posture and how you sit in relation to the other person

- active listening (this will be covered in greater depth later in this chapter).

KEY REFLECTIONS

- How can you tell when you have 'rapport' with another person?
- How do you build rapport with someone when you are working with them for the first time?

OBSERVING THE SIGNS OF RAPPORT ... OR THE LACK OF IT!

If you would like to explore the signs of rapport in more detail, pay attention to what is taking place next time you are with someone whose company you enjoy:

- What do you observe about their body language?
- What do you observe about your own body language?
- How do you feel when you are with this person?

Repeat these observations when you are with someone whose company you do not enjoy. What, if any, differences can you observe?

CASE STUDY: PAUL

Paul is training to be a teacher and has arrived at School A for his first placement. He knows that one of his university tutors will be visiting him and has been introduced to the teacher who will be his mentor. She has told him that she will be having an initial meeting with him that afternoon – he is nervous as he knows she will be assessing his practice whilst he is on placement and she will therefore affect his ability to progress, or not, as a trainee teacher.

He is not sure what he will be expected to do and is worried about being watched and assessed on a regular basis. He has started to wonder why he decided to train as a teacher.

CASE STUDY REFLECTIONS

- As his mentor, when and where should you meet with Paul?
- How can you ensure that Paul understands the roles of mentor and mentee?

As Paul's mentor, you should meet with him as soon as you can after he joins the school and, preferably, somewhere where you can talk without being disturbed. You might want to show him the staff room and the areas/classrooms he will be working in, and then sit him down in a quieter area. If you ask him if he would like a hot or cold drink (and maybe even provide some biscuits!) that will help to create a friendly and less formal atmosphere.

If you are sitting at a table, sit alongside (or, if it's a small table, at 90 degrees to) Paul to help him to see this as a more collaborative discussion. If you sit opposite him, this will add some formality to the occasion and could even seem like an interview, which might make him more nervous.

You could then introduce yourself, and explain what your role is and how you will be working with him. Then, before discussing the mentor/mentee roles and relationship, smile and ask him to tell you about himself and what led him to train as a teacher. This will demonstrate your interest in him as a person and will help to build rapport between you. Once he has finished telling you his story, tell him a little about yourself and your teaching career.

Then ask him what he knows about how mentoring works in schools, to check his existing understanding – he might not know anything but this will help you to address any misconceptions he may have and to build upon what he does know.

Depending upon the time available, you may want to have your contracting discussion at this point or at another scheduled time in the same week. At that meeting, follow the same seating arrangement if you can and then discuss your expectations of each other – Paul may be reluctant to say too much at first, but keep encouraging him to think about what he wants to learn during his placement and to express his opinions.

ACTiVE LiSTENiNG

Active listening requires a mentor to attend to every signal the mentee gives, verbal and non-verbal, and to synthesise this information to search for meaning (Zeus and Skiffington, 2002). It underpins a mentor's ability to develop rapport and provide effective support for their mentee (Downey, 2014; Tolhurst, 2010; Starr, 2016). There is a difference between hearing and listening: hearing is a passive response, which does not require any comprehension of what the other person is saying, whilst listening requires the listener to focus and seek to understand.

Thomas and Smith (2009, p.47) suggest that we need to be aware of our own ego as not having such awareness can lead to 'favoured listening' – that is, hearing what we want to hear. How we listen is affected by our personal reaction to what we have just heard (see the earlier consideration of our own values and beliefs in this chapter) which affects the clarity of the message we receive.

Listening is a complex task, but the overall outcome is to understand your mentee's meaning. Good listening skills include:

- paying attention: to verbal and non-verbal signals; allowing people to finish what they are saying

- checking your understanding: paraphrasing, summarising and/or reflecting back the mentee's words

- allowing silence: do not rush in or interrupt; allow the mentee to reflect during the silence

- encouraging exploration: make it clear that you want to support the mentee and hear their story by saying, for example: 'Tell me more about that.'

Identify your usual listening style by using the Approaches to Listening continuum shown in Figure 6.2.

HELPFUL APPROACHES	UNHELPFUL APPROACHES
Asking what the person is thinking or feeling	Mind reading
Letting the person finish their thought before you formulate your next question	Rehearsing
Being aware of your own assumptions	Filtering
Staying present	Daydreaming
Remembering it's about them not you	Identifying
Treating each person as unique	Comparing
Staying focused	Derailing
Understanding their reality before moving forward	Fixing

Figure 6.2   Approaches to Listening continuum

Most people, however experienced they are as mentors, will be closer to some of the 'helpful approaches' than others. Bear your responses in mind next time you are in a mentoring discussion. Active listening is a crucial factor in the effectiveness of mentoring: if you do not listen and understand what your mentee is saying, how can you ask them questions and know how best to support them?

QUESTIONING

Questions help a mentee to explore their behaviour and thinking, encouraging them to identify their goals and potential. Questions needs to be clear, open, focused, thought-provoking and lead to learning (Rogers, 2012). According to Thomas and

Smith (2009, p.116), such questions uncover truth, clarify meaning, test commitment and open avenues of thought.

Two well-known categories of question are:

- *Open questions*: these encourage your mentee to think and reflect. They require longer answers than closed questions (see below) and can enable your mentee's creative thinking by giving them the space to think of strategies and actions they have not previously considered. Open questions give control to the mentee and will often begin with:
  - What?
  - When?
  - How?
  - Who?
  - Where?

  Whilst it is common, in general conversation, to start an open question with 'Why' there are many authors – including Downey (2014), Thomas and Smith (2009), Whitmore (2009) and Davies (2016) – who advise against its use, suggesting that starting a question with 'Why' can create defensiveness and encourage a mentee to come up with excuses rather than considered responses.

- *Closed questions*: these require a short answer, often 'Yes' or 'No'. For example, 'Is that correct?' or 'Did you work at that school?' Closed questions can be useful when you are seeking clarification or checking your understanding – they are quick and easy to answer, and give control to the mentor rather than the mentee. Therefore, when helping a mentee to learn and develop, the majority of your questions should be open.

You can help your mentee to reflect by asking questions and giving prompts such as:

- 'Can you give me an example of ...?'
- 'To what extent ...?'
- 'Are you suggesting ...?'
- 'How do you know that?'
- 'Tell me more about ...'

Other useful types of question, as listed by Thomas and Smith (2009, p.121), include:

- *Future placing questions*: 'What will it be like in six months' time?'

- *Truth-probers*: 'What's stopping you?'

- *Short and simple questions*: 'What do you want?'

- *Reframing questions* can move a negative to a positive, and help to stop 'all or nothing' thinking. Reframing shifts things from a problem focus to a solution focus – for example, if a mentee says 'I'm no good at teaching', you could ask questions such as: 'What aspects of teaching can you do?' 'What's stopping you from being good at teaching?' 'What would good teaching look like?'

- *Incisive questions*: these place the mentee in an envisioned future where any perceived barriers to progress have been removed. For example, if time has been mentioned as a barrier, you could say 'Imagine that time isn't an issue – what would you do next ...?' which can help to shift your mentee into a more positive and action-focused mindset.

- *Commitment questions*: 'What will you do and when will you do it?'

- *Distal questions*: can be asked at the end of a mentoring session with a request that the mentee thinks about these questions and comes back to the next mentoring session with their thoughts and reflections.

If you are particularly interested in questioning, see the 'reflective practice' and 'process models' sections in Chapter 7.

KEY REFLECTIONS

- Which of the above question types do you use when mentoring? Which do you use the most and which do you use the least (or never)? Once you have a clear picture of this, try to use more of the lowest rated types of question and see what impact they have upon your mentoring.

- Next time you are about to ask a question starting with 'Why', reword the sentence so that it starts with one of the other words shown above and see what happens. For example, 'Why did you do that?' could change to 'What led to your decision to take that approach?' or 'How did that happen?'

CASE STUDY: CHANTELLE

Chantelle was in her first year of teaching and had been allocated a new mentor as her previous one had changed school. At their first meeting, Chantelle described a classroom situation that she did not know how to deal with and wanted her mentor to give her some advice on how she could address it. Her first mentor gave her a lot of advice and would do most of the talking during a mentoring session. However, instead of giving her advice, her new mentor asked her a question: 'You've been teaching for almost a year now – what strategies have you used in the past that might be useful in this situation?'

Chantelle was used to a more directive type of mentoring so was momentarily speechless as this was not what she was expecting. She responded with 'I don't know – what do you think?' in an attempt to return to the type of relationship that was more familiar to her.

CASE STUDY REFLECTIONS

What would you do if you were Chantelle's mentor?

What would be the benefits and disadvantages, for Chantelle, of:

- giving your advice when she asked for it?
- repeating your question to help her come up with her own ideas?

The best approach to take, as Chantelle's mentor, would be to repeat the question you had asked her. If you do what she wants you to do, and give her your advice, you are setting a precedent for the rest of your mentoring relationship – a precedent that would not be to Chantelle's benefit as it will not help her to think for herself. Your role is to encourage her to draw upon her previous experiences and on the reading and/or research that she has done. Only when she has done this, and has been prompted to think of one more idea, should you give your advice.

SUMMARISING

You can summarise what your mentee has said, at various stages during a discussion, as this will show that you have listened to your mentee and will enable you to check that you have accurately understood your mentee's meaning.

When summarising, you give a short verbal summary of the main points made by your mentee. A couple of useful ways to start a sentence would be:

- 'Can I summarise what you've said? I think you said ...'

- 'Can I just check ...?'

It can also be helpful to end with 'Is that right?' or 'Have I understood you correctly?' as that gives your mentee permission to correct you.

It can be more powerful when you use the mentee's own words/phrases as, by using your own words, you are putting your own interpretation on what they have said. At its worst, this can lead to you making false assumptions and misinterpreting their meaning. For example, if an early career teacher tells you s/he finds a particular class very challenging what do you think s/he means? Does s/he find the class difficult to teach? Or is s/he saying that s/he enjoys the intellectual challenge? It is impossible to know without some additional information, so do not jump to conclusions. However, summarising or reflecting back should help to dispel any false conclusions as, once they have listened to your summary, the mentee can clarify their meaning.

At the end of a mentoring session, you could also ask your mentee to summarise any actions they have agreed to take as this would help you to check their understanding and that they have remembered those next steps. This could also enable you to see if they are acknowledging any development areas and targets you have discussed – if a mentee can articulate their goals, they are more likely to achieve them.

CHALLENGING

Being mentored should be a challenging and stretching experience (Munro Turner, 2004). Yet the extent to which you challenge a mentee needs to be carefully considered – too much can be overwhelming whilst too little can mean that the mentee is not encouraged to reach beyond their comfort zone. Your tone of voice and your body language will also affect the message you are giving them along with any challenging question ... the mentee will be weighing up whether you are genuinely keen to hear their response or whether you are being critical.

Challenging can help your mentee to develop different perspectives on, and insights into, a situation they are facing as well as their own response to it. There are various ways in which you can challenge a mentee, many of which involve questioning and all of which require a positive and established relationship:

- reframing: encouraging the mentee to explore a situation from different viewpoints

- reflecting back: usually involves repeating an exact statement, phrase or sentence that the mentee has used; when the mentee hears their own words spoken back to them they may reconsider their situation, thinking or approach

- sharing information: making the mentee aware of something they had not previously considered

- giving feedback (covered later in this chapter).

The impact of this challenge will depend upon the relationship you have developed. At an early stage, whilst the rapport is still being established, you could seek a mentee's permission to challenge them – this could be discussed as part of the contracting process. One way to introduce the concept during the contracting process would be to say: 'As part of my mentoring role I want to help you consider situations from different viewpoints so that you can gain an insight into a range of perspectives. How will you feel if I ask you questions that help you to think of things that you haven't considered before?' This introduces the idea that you will not necessarily accept everything that they say, and will help to frame their expectations of mentoring.

FEEDBACK

As a mentor, you will be giving feedback on your mentee's teaching. To have the greatest impact on their learning, it is important to consider how your feedback is delivered in terms of its wording and structure.

Here is some guidance on preparing and giving feedback to your mentee:

a) start with the positives: say what you think they did well and the impact this could have on the children and/or young adults they are teaching

b) give it with care: you want to help, not hurt, the mentee

c) pay attention: concentrate on what you are doing as you give feedback, e.g. what is your body language and your tone of voice conveying?

d) be specific: be direct, focus on specific things you observed

e) own your feedback: make it clear that any judgements are your opinion, based on what you observed, rather than being a universal truth

f) be well timed: give your feedback as soon as possible after the observed session, and deliver it in a sufficiently private location

g) discuss behaviour: focus on what they did, not who they are as a person

h) involve a two-way exchange: show that you are open to receiving, as well as giving, feedback

i) it should result in some next steps: describe things that the mentee can alter and help them to consider how they can make these changes.

KEY REFLECTIONS

Feedback:

*   Consider the above guidance on preparing and giving feedback: is there anything missing? If so, add it to the list. Then tick the items that relate to your current practice and put a cross by those that do not.

*   Rate yourself against each element: 1 (I do not do this or I am not very good at this); 2 (I am okay but could do better); 3 (I am good at this).

*   Then share your views with someone who is familiar with your mentoring approach and ask what their perceptions are of the way in which you mentor trainees/colleagues. Or, if you are feeling particularly brave, you could ask them to rate your practice against each aspect, and then compare their perceptions to your own.

Your mentoring skills:

*   What do you consider to be your strengths and areas for development in terms of mentoring skills?

*   How do you/could you collect information on your mentoring skills?

*   What can you do to address your areas for development and who/what can support you?

CHAPTER SUMMARY

*   Most government publications on school-based mentoring do not specify the skills that enable effective mentoring.

- Every mentor will have a different combination of strengths and areas for development.

- Effective mentoring is tailored to each mentee and will work towards enabling them to come up with their own solutions and way forward.

- A mentor's values and beliefs will influence the way in which they mentor – it is therefore important to be aware of one's own, as well as the mentee's, values and beliefs as they will affect your attitudes to teaching and learning.

- A contracting discussion is an essential foundation for a mentoring relationship: one which clarifies roles and expectations of each other. Both the mentor and mentee should contribute to this agreement.

- The environment, and the approach taken during this discussion, will have a significant impact on the building of rapport and trust between both parties.

- The quality of the mentor's listening, questioning, summarising, challenging and feedback skills will have an impact on their mentee's self-awareness, decision-making and development as a trainee or early career teacher.

SELF-AUDIT QUESTIONS

- Which mentoring skills were covered within this chapter?

- Which of these skills creates the basis for all future mentoring discussions with a mentee?

- Who created the Spectrum of Coaching model included in this chapter?

- When asking an open question, which word do we suggest you avoid starting a question with and for what reasons?

SUGGESTED FURTHER READING

Clutterbuck, D. (2014) *Everyone Needs A Mentor*. London: Chartered Institute of Personnel and Development (CIPD).

Garvey, B., Stokes, P. and Megginson, D. (2009) *Coaching and Mentoring: Theory and Practice.* London: SAGE.

Iordanou, I., Hawley, R. and Iordanou, C. (2017) *Values and Ethics in Coaching.* London: SAGE.

Kline, N. (1999) *Time to Think: Listening to Ignite the Human Mind.* London: Octopus.

Pask, R. and Joy, B. (2007) *Mentoring-Coaching: A Guide for Education Professionals.* Berkshire: Open University Press.

Starr, J. (2014) *The Mentoring Manual: Your Step-by-Step Guide to Being a Better Mentor.* Harlow: Pearson.

Thomas, W. and Smith, A. (2009) *Coaching Solutions: Practical Ways to Improve Performance in Education.* London: Network Continuum.

REFERENCES

Argyris, C. (1990) *Overcoming Organizational Defenses: Facilitating Organizational Learning.* New Jersey: Prentice Hall.

Clutterbuck, D. (2014) *Everyone Needs A Mentor.* London: Chartered Institute of Personnel and Development (CIPD).

Clutterbuck, D. (2018) *LinkedIn.* 5 May. Available at https://www.linkedin.com/in/prof-david-clutterbuck-84aa6b/detail/recent-activity/posts/ (accessed: 5 May 2018).

Connor, M. and Pokora, J. (2012) *Coaching and Mentoring at Work.* Berkshire: Open University Press.

Corradi, F. (1990) *The Other Side of Language.* New York: Routledge.

Davies, P. (2016) *A Short Introduction to Coaching Skills and the GROW Model.* Independently published.

Department for Education (DfE) (2018) *Strengthening Qualified Teacher Status Etc.: Government Consultation Response May 2018.* Available at https://www.gov.uk/government/consultations/strengthening-qualified-teacher-status-and-career-progression (accessed: 16 April 2019).

Downey, M. (1999) *Effective Coaching: Lessons from the Coaches' Coach.* London: LID.

Downey, M. (2014) *Effective Modern Coaching.* London: LID.

Flaherty, J. (2010) *Coaching: Evoking Excellence in Others.* London: Butterworth-Heinemann.

Lancer, N., Clutterbuck, D. and Megginson, D. (2016) *Techniques for Coaching and Mentoring.* Oxfordshire: Routledge.

Lenz, A. (2014) Mediating effects of relationships with mentors on college adjustment. *Journal of College Counselling*, 17195-207.

Munro Turner (2004) Values and Beliefs. *Coaching Today*. Available at https://www.mikethe mentor.co.uk/blog/values-and-beliefs (accessed 16 April 2019).

Oxford Living Dictionaries (2019) https://en.oxforddictionaries.com/definition/belief (accessed 16 April 2019).

Parsloe, J. and Leedham, M. (2016) *Coaching and Mentoring: Practical Techniques for Developing Learning and Performance*. London: Kogan Page.

Pask, R. and Joy, B. (2007) *Mentoring-Coaching: A Guide for Education Professionals*. Berkshire: Open University Press.

Rogers, J. (2012) *Coaching Skills: A Handbook*. Berkshire: Open University Press.

Starr, J. (2016) *The Coaching Manual*. Edinburgh: Pearson Education.

Teaching Schools Council (2016) *National Standards for School-Based Initial Teacher Training (ITT) Mentors*. Available at https://assets.publishing.service.gov.uk/government/uploads/ system/uploads/attachment_data/file/536891/Mentor_standards_report_Final.pdf (accessed 17 April 2019).

Thomas, W. and Smith, A. (2009) *Coaching Solutions: Practical Ways to Improve Performance in Education*. London: Network Continuum.

Tolhurst, J. (2010) *The Essential Guide to Coaching and Mentoring: Practical Skills for Teachers*. Harlow: Longman/Pearson Education.

VIA Institute on Character (2019). *The VIA Survey*. Available at https://www.viacharacter.org/ www/Character-Strengths-Survey (accessed 16 April 2019).

Whitmore, J. (2009) *Coaching for Performance: GROWing Human Potential and Purpose: the Principles and Practice of Coaching and Leadership*. London: Nicholas Brealey.

Zeus, P. and Skiffington, S. (2002) *The Coaching at Work Toolkit: A Complete Guide to Techniques and Practices*. Sydney: McGraw-Hill.

MODELS AND TECHNIQUES FOR MENTORING

7

CHAPTER OBJECTIVES

By the end of this chapter you should be aware of:

- a range of techniques that you could use to support your mentees reflections, decision-making and practice

- some process models that can help you to structure your mentoring conversations

- the therapeutic sources of some of these process models and techniques. This will enable you to explore these sources in further depth, should you wish, through wider reading including the titles listed at the end of this chapter under suggested further reading.

MENTOR STANDARDS

This chapter supports the development of the following Mentor Standards (Teaching Schools Council, 2016, p.10):

- Standard 1 – Personal qualities: Establish trusting relationships, modelling high standards of practice, and empathising with the challenges a trainee faces.

- Standard 2 – Teaching: Support trainees to develop their teaching practice in order to set high expectations and to meet the needs of all pupils.

- Standard 3 – Professionalism: Induct the trainee into professional norms and values, helping them to understand the importance of the role and responsibilities of teachers in society.

- Standard 4 – Self-development and working in partnership: Continue to develop their own professional knowledge, skills and understanding and invest time in developing a good working relationship within relevant ITT partnerships.

iNTRODUCTiON

This chapter will focus upon some models and techniques that you can use to aid your mentees' thinking, development and teaching. Your application of these models and techniques will help your mentees to gain an insight into their thinking, reflect upon their practice, gain an overview of their situation, set priorities and make informed decisions.

It provides an introduction to a range of models and techniques that you can use when supporting, challenging and empowering your mentees. Some will be appropriate whatever the stage of a mentee's journey, whilst others may be best suited to trainee teachers and those in the early stages of their teaching career. It is up to you to tailor your approach with each of your mentees and it is our hope that the contents of this chapter provide you with some models and techniques that you may like to use.

The models and techniques covered within this chapter will help you to:

- extend your mentee's self-awareness

- raise awareness of their thought processes

- develop their informed decision-making

- aid their reflective practice

- reduce barriers that mentees may be placing in their own path

- assist your mentees with the development of their own goals.

Some of the approaches discussed have emerged from theoretical frameworks that inform mentoring and coaching, such as cognitive behavioural therapy, motivational interviewing, positive psychology and solution-focused coaching. If you would like to explore these approaches in more depth, suggestions for further reading sources may be found at the end of this chapter. Many of the models and techniques within this chapter focus upon developing the mentee's self-awareness and, hopefully, your own.

THE ROLE OF PSYCHOMETRIC TESTS

You can help your mentees to learn more about themselves by encouraging them to complete some of the online exercises available to them free of charge, such as the VIA Character Strengths Inventory (VIA Institute on Character, 2019) mentioned in Chapter 6. Some psychometric tests are freely available to anyone with internet access whilst a range of others will be available to your mentees if they are linked to an educational institution that has subscribed to some costed resources.

A discussion about your mentee's results (and possibly your own results if you also complete the psychometric test) – possibly focusing upon areas of similarity and areas of difference, and what they could mean for ways in which you approach situations and each other – could provide you with a non-threatening way to discuss your different perceptions and approaches.

Trainee teachers linked to a higher education institution (HEI) can also benefit from a variety of psychometric tests that their HEI subscribes to. One example, which some HEIs subscribe to, is the Profiling for Success Type Dynamics Indicator which helps the user to understand their preferences in the workplace. The report, sent to the user after they have completed the online test, includes coverage of:

- why you work
- the kind of work you want
- your style of working
- the type of people you want to work with
- how others might view you
- your main assets
- areas to consider developing.

If your mentee is willing to share this report with you, it can provide a means by which you can discuss their perceptions and preferred approaches whilst you are building a mentoring relationship with them. However, it is worth noting that the report will talk about ways in which the mentee *might* behave in a specific situation rather than what they will actually do.

CONTRACTING

Though contracting has already been covered in Chapter 6, it is mentioned again in this chapter due to its importance as a technique as well as a key skill. If, at the start of your mentoring relationship, you and your mentee agree upon your expectations of each other, you can return to this contract (which might benefit from being written down in some way) if one of you is not keeping to that agreement. For example, if you clarify that you (as the mentor) expect your mentee to reflect upon their practice and identify its strengths and weaknesses – rather than solely relying on you for advice and feedback – you can revisit this contract (making sure, of course, that you have provided your mentee with sufficient guidance and tools – maybe those shown later in this chapter – to enable them to reflect!) if they are not doing so.

OPENING YOUR MENTORING DISCUSSIONS

We cannot overstate the importance of meeting the mentee's needs as well as covering any aspects that you, as the mentor, want to cover during a discussion.

Asking your mentee 'What would you like to take away from our discussion today?' or 'What would make you feel that our discussion was valuable today?' will signal that you are keen to hear what they have to say and that you want to support their development.

Do not be too disappointed if your mentee does not identify anything the first time you ask them this question … they might be surprised and rendered speechless for a short while! But if you keep asking this question each time you meet, the mentee will start to reflect before the sessions as they will know that you are expecting them to help shape the agenda.

> KEY REFLECTIONS: OPENING YOUR MENTORING DISCUSSIONS
>
> • How do you currently open each of your mentoring discussions?
> • Who sets the agenda for these discussions?

THE JOHARI WINDOW (1955)

The Johari Window was developed by Luft and Ingham in 1955 with the aim of helping people to enhance their self-awareness. It is also linked to reflective practice as it encourages us to consider what we know about ourselves; what others might know about us that we already know/do not know; and facets that neither we nor anyone else know about ourselves.

1		2
Known Self Things we know about ourselves and others know about us		**Hidden Self** Things we know about ourselves that others do not know
3		4
Blind Self Things others know about us that we do not know		**Unknown Self** Things neither we nor others know about us

Figure 7.1   Johari Window

Figure 7.1, shown above, depicts the Johari Window. As you can see, it has four quadrants:

- *Known self*: what you know about yourself that others also know about you

- *Hidden self*: what you know about yourself but that you hide from other people

- *Blind self*: what others know about you but that you do not know about yourself

- *Unknown self*: what no-one knows about you (not even yourself).

This model can aid the mentoring process as it provides a (hopefully) non-threatening way of explaining to your mentees that they do not know everything about themselves. They have their own knowledge about themselves, and others (including you as their mentor) can add insights/perceptions that can help them to have a more complete picture of who they are.

REFLECTiVE PRACTiCE

Though mentioned at various points within this book, this chapter considers a model that can help your mentee to become familiar with reflective practice. From a mentoring viewpoint, reflective practice can help a mentee (and a mentor) in a variety of ways, including:

- seeing things from more than one perspective, e.g. seeking to understand why someone (or even a class) might have behaved in a certain way

- considering how your past experiences can affect the ways in which you think and behave

- recognising that you have a choice in how you think and act

- recognising that you can change your views and your behaviour

- seeing the 'bigger picture'

- considering how you can use this learning and understanding to inform your future thoughts and behaviour.

Though numerous models of reflective practice exist, this chapter will focus upon one seminal model: Gibbs' reflective cycle (1988).

GiBBS' REFLECTIVE CYCLE (1988)

Gibbs' six-stage reflective model, shown at Figure 7.2, was initially developed for teachers, and aims to help people learn from situations they face on a regular basis.

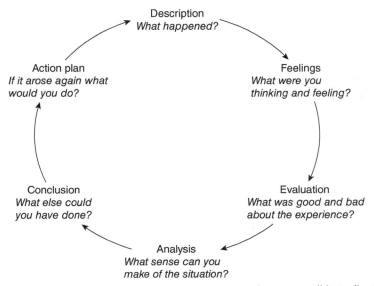

Figure 7.2   Gibbs' reflective cycle (1988)

Starting with 'Description', at the top of the cycle, Gibbs' reflective cycle encourages the user to follow a process which enables them not only to think about a situation, but also to consider a wider range of aspects, use these reflections to analyse what happened and use this information to decide what to do in the future.

The following template is based upon Gibbs' reflective cycle (1988). If you transfer it to a blank sheet, and create larger text boxes below each heading, your mentee could use it to reflect on a situation they have faced – for example, a lesson they have taught.

Consider a recent experience/situation and note your responses *Why did you choose this example to focus upon?*
Description *What happened? Just describe at this point (don't include judgements, feelings or conclusions at this stage).*
Feeling *What were you thinking and feeling whilst it was happening, and what were your reactions to these thoughts and feelings?*
Evaluation *What was good about this experience? What was bad about this experience?*
Analysis *What sense can you make of this situation? What do you think was really going on?*
Conclusion *What have you concluded about this experience? What else could you have done?*
Action plan *What would you do the same next time/what would you do differently?*

Figure 7.3   Reflective cycle template

If reflective practice is not a familiar concept to your mentee, you could put some phrases on the other side of the sheet which they could use to start some of their reflective sentences:

- 'I think …'
- 'I feel …'
- 'I could have …'
- 'I think/feel it went well because …'
- 'In hindsight I could have …'
- 'In future I will try to …'

As a mentor, you might want to try some reflective practice yourself if you are not doing it on a regular basis already. This might help to shed some light on situations that you have found particularly difficult when working with a mentee.

Maybe you could set up a community of practice for mentors in your institution in which you can all share your reflections and ideas.

PROCESS MODELS

There are various process models – such as GROW (Whitmore, 1992), OSCAR (2002), STRIDE (Thomas and Smith, 2009) and FUEL (Zenger and Stinnett, 2010) – that can help you to structure your mentoring discussions. Many of these models have similar elements but use different names for each stage of the process. Most start with the identification of the mentee's goal, followed by an exploration of what is currently going on in relation to that aspect, a consideration of possible options and then an action planning/target setting stage. Some models follow this with a review stage as a reminder that you need to review the action plan/targets with your mentee at the next meeting.

Two models that are particularly popular within the education sector are GROW (Whitmore, 1992) and STRIDE (Thomas and Smith, 2009), both of which are outlined below.

THE GROW MODEL (1992)

The four-step GROW model (1992) provides a framework for a discussion through which you can help your mentee to explore a specific situation, identify their priorities, set goals and identify how they can achieve these goals.

Under each of the four steps shown below, we have included examples of questions that might be asked. You are not meant to use each of these questions in turn – we have included them to give you some understanding of what might be asked. It is only when you are in the mentoring discussion that you will know what your mentee will say and this will guide your choice of questions ... remember you are having a conversation, not reading from a script!

1. **Goal**

    - What do you want to achieve?

    - What part of this is most important to you?

    - What will be happening when you have reached your goal?

    - How will things differ from the way they are now?

2. **Reality**

    - What is going on at the moment?

- What happened?

- What have you tried?

- What have you learned?

3. **Options**

- What could you do?

- What else could you do?

- What are the advantages and disadvantages of each option?

- What could you do if you had more time/more funding/greater power?

4. **Will**

- What will you do?

- What will your first step be?

- When will you do that?

- What support will you need and from whom?

THE STRIDE MODEL (2009)

The six-step STRIDE model pays particular attention to a mentee's strengths, and also to the evaluation of their commitment to their decisions/actions and to a follow-up discussion. We have included examples of potential questions under each heading.

The six steps are:

1. **Strengths**

- What strengths do you have that could help you in this situation?

- What has helped you to succeed in the past?

- What would your best friend say is your greatest strength?

2. **Target**

- What do you want?

- What excites you about this?

- How will you know when you have achieved this target/goal?

3. **Real situation**

- What is going on at the moment?

- What is missing?

- What have you already tried?

- What is stopping you?

[If your mentee is feeling negative, you could prompt them by asking: 'What strengths do you have that could help you at this point?']

4. **Ideas**

- What can you do to reach your target?

- What would you do if there was nothing standing in your way?

5. **Decision**

- What will you do?

- When will you do it?

- How will this get you closer to your target?

6. **Evaluation**

- The decision: exploring the mentee's commitment to their decision

- Follow-up: arranging a time to discuss the steps taken by the mentee after this decision was made.

Focusing upon and recognising a mentee's strengths can help to enhance their self-esteem, encourage a positive mindset and develop rapport between you. Thomas and Smith (2009) recommend the use of strength identification throughout the STRIDE process, promoting its use as a powerful and valuable tool for both mentor and mentee.

Even though these models can provide a useful framework for mentors who are relatively new to the concept, they are not meant to be deployed 'in a slavishly linear fashion ... they are designed as broad checklists' (McLeod and Thomas, 2010, p.198). As these process models are encouraging your mentee to reflect on their situation and to consider their next steps they are – in some ways – similar to the reflective practice models mentioned earlier in this chapter.

ACTION PLANNING/TARGET SETTING

Most process models conclude with an action planning stage as, towards the end of a mentoring conversation, you will be encouraging your mentee to consider some areas for development.

Your mentee's targets need to be as clear and detailed as possible, and you could use the following SMART questions as a checklist against which to assess each draft target:

- **S**PECIFIC: is it sufficiently detailed so the mentee knows exactly what they are meant to do?

- **M**EASURABLE: can its achievement be measured/will we know if it has been achieved or not?

- **A**DVANTAGES: what are the advantages of achieving this target?

- **R**EALISTIC: how realistic is it?

- **T**IMESCALE: is there a deadline?

Remember that, as well as addressing areas for development, you can ask a mentee to build upon their strengths – this can help with motivation and confidence building as you are not solely focusing upon what the mentee is lacking.

MENTORING WHEEL

Sometimes there is so much going on that it is difficult for a mentee to identify what their focus could or should be. One way of helping them to gain a clearer picture is to use a mentoring wheel. Put simply, this is a circle divided into equal-sized segments depending upon the number of items you want it to include: maybe six, eight or ten items.

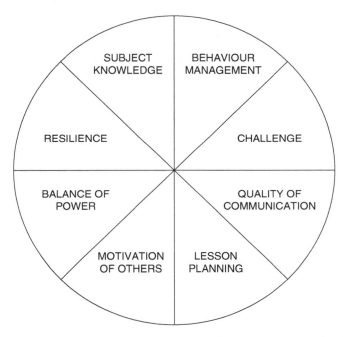

Figure 7.4   An example of a mentoring wheel

The labels shown in Figure 7.4 are examples: you and your mentee can decide upon the labels that are best suited to your mentoring focus at that point.

Each section of the wheel has a scale of 0–10: 0 (at the centre) represents total dissatisfaction and 10 (at the outside) represents total satisfaction.

Your mentee would decide upon their satisfaction with each aspect and then shade in the segment to that point – for example, if they rated their behaviour management skills as a 5, the segment would be shaded to the half-way point.

After following this process for each aspect, the mentee would have a visual depiction of their levels of satisfaction with various important aspects of their situation and could then identify – possibly in collaboration with you as their mentor – what they need to focus upon.

THE BLOB TREE (2015)

You may already be familiar with the Blob Tree drawing and may have used it in the classroom or when supporting colleagues. For those of you who do not recognise the name, it depicts a tree populated by various blob-like characters.

Some people find it easier, and more comfortable, to identify how they feel by considering a visual prompt (such as the Blob Tree) rather than by being asked to describe their feelings. If you ask your mentee to identify which character most closely resembles how they feel at that moment in time (or in a specific situation) it can help them to quickly identify that state.

Once your mentee has identified the character that represents their current state of mind, you could ask your mentee to explain their reasons for selecting this drawing. Do not make any assumptions based upon the drawing – your perceptions may differ from those of your mentee so always ask them to describe their reasons for selecting that particular one. This will then give you the basis for a further discussion and exploration of their feelings and thoughts.

KEY REFLECTIONS: THE BLOB TREE

- Have you seen the Blob Tree before? If so, how was it used?
- Is it something that you would like to use within your mentoring discussions?

THREE GOOD THINGS

As its name implies, positive psychology is a positive approach which assumes that individuals can find their own solutions and have the internal resources required to change. Rather than focusing upon what is not going well, and getting caught up in the 'problems', you can help your mentee to identify and build upon their strengths. The VIA Character Strengths Inventory, mentioned in Chapter 6, is an example of a positive psychology approach.

Positive psychology can be particularly helpful when you are working with a mentee whose negativity, or self-doubt, makes it difficult for them to see things in perspective. As well as examining and challenging thinking patterns, you can encourage them to set and work towards small goals, explore instances when they were successful/resilient and help them to visualise their future achievements (Hefferon, 2011).

One positive psychology approach is to focus upon 'three good things'. If you find that your mentee (or you) are spending too much time on the negative aspects of their performance, you can ask them to identify three good things that happened during that day, or during their teaching practice, to help set a more positive tone (Kauffman et al., 2014).

LIMITING BELIEFS

As mentioned in Chapter 6, beliefs are ideas that we no longer question. They provide us with an internal guide to how we think, how we behave and how we reach decisions. Whilst some of these beliefs are helpful, others can hinder our progress. In many cases, we are making assumptions about things without any proof of their reality.

Listening to a mentee, and asking them questions about their thinking and behaviour, can help you to identify beliefs that may be limiting their personal and professional development. Bandler and Grinder (1975) identify three different types of limiting beliefs:

- *Distortions*: imagining what someone else might be thinking. Examples: 'He doesn't like me'; 'She doesn't want me to get the job.'

- *Generalisations*: sweeping generalisations which are applied to someone's behaviour, every situation or a group of people. Examples: 'She always speaks over me in meetings'; 'I can't do that.' They may include the use of words such as 'never', 'everyone' and 'always'.

- *Deletions*: making comparisons with something that is not specified. Examples: 'That's too expensive'; 'That's too hard.'

If you help your mentee to identify any of these limiting beliefs you will be helping them to consider alternative ways of thinking and to change a limiting belief to one that is more positive.

Based on the examples shown above, here are some ways in which you could help your mentee to reframe their limiting beliefs:

Distortions:

Mentee: 'He doesn't like me'

Mentor: 'How do you know he doesn't like you?'

Mentee: 'She doesn't want me to get the job'

Mentor: 'How do you know she doesn't want you to get the job?'

Generalisations:

    Mentee: 'She always speaks over me in meetings'

    Mentor: 'Always?'

    Mentee: 'I can't do that'

    Mentor: 'Which parts of that can you do?'

Deletions:

    Mentee: 'That's too expensive/too hard'

    Mentor: 'Compared to what?'

THE ABC MODEL (1957)

If your mentee lacks confidence because of a previous experience, and is finding it difficult to move forward and try again, you could use a technique that has been adapted from cognitive behavioural therapy (CBT). The ABC model (Ellis, 1957) is based on the idea that our thoughts affect our emotions and our behaviour. The following case study aims to provide an insight into how this model may be used within a mentoring situation. Read the case study and consider implications for mentoring this person.

CASE STUDY: MARTHA

A: *Activating activity/adversity*: Martha's lesson did not go as well as she had hoped and she became flustered when some of the pupils started laughing.

B: *Beliefs*: Martha believed that she had lost her credibility with the class and that they would not take her seriously again.

C: *Consequences*: as a consequence, Martha felt like a fool and had the following thoughts: 'They're laughing at me and won't respect me after this.' 'I can't go into a classroom again.'

CASE STUDY REFLECTIONS

- What are the triggers for Martha feeling the way she does?

- What techniques might you use as her mentor?

Martha is clearly concerned by her lesson not going well and the impact it will have on her future in teaching. She is distressed by the pupils' responses. Whilst her reaction is understandable, you can remind Martha that she has choices and has chosen to believe that she has lost her credibility and that the pupils will not take her seriously again. Her beliefs have influenced her thoughts and these will have consequences for her.

You could ask Martha to consider the same scenario but to adopt a different set of beliefs:

- A: *Activating activity/adversity*: a lesson did not go as planned and Martha became flustered when some of the pupils started laughing.

- B: *Beliefs*: Martha has become a bit flustered, but believes that this is normal for someone who is training to be a teacher. She views this as an opportunity to learn how to manage a class when under pressure, something that she will need to do on many occasions in a teaching career.

- C: *Consequences*: as a consequence, Martha felt annoyed but was also determined to learn and improve. She decided to continue with the lesson once the laughter had died down.

You could use the ABC model to talk through other situations that your mentee has found difficult, exploring the choices they made in terms of their beliefs and reactions. Realising that they have choices, rather than being steered solely by events, can help a mentee to take more control over their emotions, thoughts and behaviour and to reduce feelings of victimhood.

Reivich and Shatte (2003) suggest there are links between particular beliefs and the emotions felt – they call these the B–C connections (see Figure 7.5).

Beliefs...	lead to...	Consequences (emotions)
• Violation of rights	→	• Anger
• Actual loss, or loss of self-worth	→	• Sadness; depression
• Future threat	→	• Anxiety; fear
• Violation of another's rights	→	• Guilt
• Loss of standing with others	→	• Embarrassment

Figure 7.5   Some common B–C connections (Reivich and Shatte, 2003)

Figure 7.5 shows how, in Reivich and Shatte's opinion, certain beliefs can lead to particular consequences in terms of emotions. For example, if you believe that there is something that could threaten you, you could experience anxiety and/or fear. As it can be easier to identify our feelings rather than our beliefs, you could use the table to explore which beliefs might be at the core of your mentee's negative emotions.

THE EMPTY CHAIR

If your mentee is talking a lot about someone else – maybe a colleague or a pupil – you might want to consider using the Empty Chair technique, which has its basis in Gestalt therapy. There are various ways in which the Empty Chair technique can be used – a couple of examples are shown in the case study below.

CASE STUDY: FAIZAL

Faizal has talked, during a number of recent mentoring sessions, about a 'difficult relationship' he has with a teaching assistant in the school. You realise that there are two sides to each story, and may therefore decide to use the Empty Chair technique to help Faizal to consider the other person's point of view.

1. Ask Faizal to move to a different chair from the one he has been sitting in during your discussion, and ask him to imagine he is the teaching assistant. Ask him some open questions to help him explore how the situation might look from the teaching assistant's viewpoint. Your mentee would start their answers with 'I think …' *or*
2. Ask Faizal to imagine the teaching assistant is sitting in the other chair, and ask him to tell the teaching assistant what is on his (the mentee's) mind.

You could combine both approaches and encourage Faizal to have a conversation with this other person whilst moving from chair to chair – that is, as Faizal, he would sit in one chair and then move to the other chair when speaking as the teaching assistant. At the end, you could ask your mentee to imagine that he is hovering above this conversation and ask him to tell you what he has observed. This can sometimes help a mentee to be more objective and to gain some additional insights into how their own thoughts and behaviour may be affecting the relationship.

CASE STUDY REFLECTIONS

The Empty Chair approach will work better with some mentees than with others. When using it for the first time, use it with someone who you have built good rapport with – you may also wish to explain that this is an experiment as you have not asked anyone to use this approach before. Say that you think it may be helpful and that you and your mentee can learn together about how this approach can work.

SCALING

Scaling can be used in many ways within a mentoring discussion. Here are some of the ways in which it can help you and your mentee.

Commitment to a course of action that you have discussed. You could say: 'On a scale from 0 to 10 – where 0 is very unlikely and 10 is very likely – how likely is it that you will do x?' This is a simple way to check your mentee's commitment and confidence in their next steps. Another way that you could phrase it is to say 'On a scale from 0 to 10, how important do you think it is for you to do x?'

If your mentee gives a low score (below 7), discuss how the steps could be more achievable or ask them what action(s) would be more significant for them (as maybe they have been telling you what they think you want to hear!). If the mentee says 7 or 8, then you could ask them what needs to happen to take their response to a 10.

Checking your mentee's meaning. When one person uses a word it can have a different meaning to what we mean when we use the same word. For example, if your mentee says that something will be 'challenging' for them, that could have a positive connotation ('this will be "challenging" for me as it will stretch me, and I'm excited by it') or a negative connotation ('this will be "challenging" for me, and I'm terrified by it') … you need to check exactly what they mean.

Here is one way to explore your mentee's meaning without making your own assumptions. If your mentee says that they would like to be more assertive, you could ask them:

- what 0 on the assertiveness scale would look like

- what 10 on the scale would look like

- where they would place themselves on their scale and what this currently looks like

- where they would like to be on the scale and what that would look like.

You could then discuss what they can do to take them from where they are now on the scale to where they would like to be.

RESISTANCE TO CHANGE

If your mentee is resisting something that they must do, rather than something which is just a difference in opinion between yourselves, you might want to consider using some techniques that form part of the motivational interviewing approach (Miller and Rollnick, 2002).

Your mentee's resistance might present itself through ignoring you, denying the reality of the situation, or arguing with you.

When faced with this scenario, you have a number of different options some of which are outlined below. Wherever possible, stay calm and avoid arguing, challenging, criticising or analysing the situation as these could make the mentee even more resistant. Some options you could try are:

- *Reflecting back*: it can help your mentee to hear their words spoken by someone else so repeat, word for word, what you heard them say. Speak calmly and do your best to remove any note of emotion or disagreement from your voice. After you have repeated their words, pause … and wait for your mentee to speak. They may start to reconsider their stance.

- *Shifting focus*: you can defuse the tension by shifting the focus of the discussion to the future – for example:

  o Mentee: 'I can't imagine not starting my lessons in that way. All of my friends do the same thing.'

  o Mentor: 'It's hard to imagine giving up something you're used to. I'm wondering, what can you imagine it will be like?'

- *Reframing*: you can help your mentee to put things in a more positive light so that they can start to consider the benefits as well as the drawbacks – for example:

  o Mentee: 'It's going to be hard for me to start my lessons in a more authoritative manner. It's not who I am.'

  o Mentor: 'Whilst it will be hard for you to do this, you're determined to do it as it will help you to control the children's behaviour so that they can all focus upon what they're learning.'

- *Considering the 'pros and cons'*: another way of helping your mentee to reach a decision about what to do next is to help them to undertake a cost/benefit analysis of their current situation and the potential change. Figure 7.6 provides one example of a matrix you could ask your mentee to complete – you could discuss this within a mentoring session or you could ask them to think about this, complete the matrix, and bring it to their next mentoring discussion.

	Continuing to do what you're currently doing	Changing to a different approach
PROS		
CONS		

Figure 7.6   Pros and cons matrix

KEY REFLECTIONS: RESISTANCE TO CHANGE

- Can you think of a mentee for whom this approach would have been helpful?
- Which of the above-mentioned options might have been most appropriate to use with that mentee?

CASE STUDY: PHILIP

Philip is in his second year of teaching, and has been successful both in terms of his teaching and his standing with colleagues. He is respected for his ability to engage the young people he teaches and for his ability to think quickly in a difficult situation.

However, during a discussion with his mentor – who he has been in a mentoring relationship with for the past year – Philip says that he feels that his apparent composure is a shell and that, underneath it all, he is struggling to maintain his interest in teaching and his energy levels. This is the first time he has mentioned these concerns to his mentor.

CASE STUDY REFLECTIONS

- How would you respond to Philip's comments?
- What might you do to help him explore his thoughts and feelings?

- Which tools/techniques might you want to use to help him clarify his thoughts?

As you have been mentoring Philip for a year, you will hopefully have built up a strong mentoring relationship and it is positive that he feels able to disclose these feelings to you.

Initially, you would want to encourage him to speak and to tell you what has led to these thoughts and feelings. Maybe they are a recent development, but maybe this is the first time he has felt able to tell you about his longstanding concerns. Sometimes being able to talk and express one's feelings is enough to help us move forward, as hearing our own words said out loud enables us to reflect upon and consider what we are actually thinking and saying.

Depending upon Philip's response, and any potential triggers that he mentions, there are a range of tools and techniques that you could use to help him consider his situation. For example:

- If a particular incident has affected his confidence, you could work through the ABC model to discuss what happened, his beliefs and how they affected how he thought and felt. You could then discuss those beliefs to help him to realise how these are affecting the choices he is making in terms of his thoughts and behaviour.

- If there are many different demands on him, and he is not sure what his priorities are for action, you could use the mentoring wheel to help him to clarify what is going on in his life/in that part of his life and what he is most and least satisfied with at present.

- You could ask him to complete the template, based on Gibbs' reflective cycle, shown earlier in this chapter, to help him to reflect upon a situation that is causing him concern. He could bring his reflections to your next mentoring session, where you could both discuss them in more detail.

KEY REFLECTIONS

- Which of the models and techniques covered within this chapter have you used?

- Which models and techniques would you like to use, and for what reasons?

- Are there any models and techniques that you are planning to find out more about?

CHAPTER SUMMARY

- There is a wide range of models and techniques that mentors can use to support, challenge and empower their mentees.

- Some models and techniques will help extend a mentee's self-awareness – particularly in relation to the way they react to situations and their own thought processes – whilst others will aid their reflective practice, help them to set their goals or reduce barriers they might be placing in their own path.

- Trainee teachers linked to an educational institution will have access to a range of psychometric tests, free of charge, which could help to increase their self-awareness.

- Many of the models and techniques shown within this chapter have emerged from therapeutic approaches.

SELF-AUDIT QUESTIONS

- What benefits can result from a mentor's use of models and techniques as part of their mentoring approach?

- Name the reflective practice model covered within this chapter.

- Name three of the therapeutic approaches that models and techniques within this chapter have emerged from.

- Which technique, mentioned within this chapter, was developed as part of the Gestalt approach?

SUGGESTED FURTHER READING

Cox, E., Bachkirova, T. and Clutterbuck, D. (2010) *The Complete Handbook of Coaching.* London: SAGE.

Law, H. (2013) *The Psychology of Coaching, Mentoring and Learning.* Chichester: Wiley Blackwell.

Palmer, S. and Whybrow, A. (2010) *Handbook of Coaching Psychology: A Guide for Practitioners.* East Sussex: Routledge.

REFERENCES

Bandler, R. and Grinder, J. (1975) *The Structure of Magic 1: A Book about Language and Therapy*. Palo Alto: Science and Behavior Books.

Ellis, A. (1957). Rational psychotherapy and individual psychology. *Journal of Individual Psychology*, 13, 38–44.

Gibbs, G. (1988). *Learning by Doing: A Guide to Teaching and Learning Methods*. Oxford: Oxford Further Education Unit.

Hefferon, K. (2011) Positive psychology. In Wildflower, L. and Brennan, D. (eds), *The Handbook of Theory Based Coaching: From Theory to Practice*. San Francisco: Jossey-Bass, pp.21–8.

Kauffman, C., Boniwell, I. and Silberman, J. (2014) The positive psychology approach to coaching. In Cox, E., Bachkirova, T. and Clutterbuck, D. (eds), *The Complete Handbook of Coaching*. London: SAGE.

Luft, J. and Ingham, H. (1955) *The Johari Window: A Graphic Model of Interpersonal Awareness*. Los Angeles: University of California Western Training Lab.

McLeod, A. and Thomas, W. (2010) *Performance Coaching Toolkit*. Maidenhead: Open University Press.

Miller, W.R. and Rollnick, S. (2002). *Motivational Interviewing: Preparing People for Change*. New York: Guilford Press.

Reivich, K. and Shatte, A. (2003) *The Resilience Factor: 7 Keys to Finding your Inner Strength and Overcoming Life's Hurdles*. New York: Three Rivers Press.

Teaching Schools Council (2016) Teaching Schools Council (2016) *National Standards for School-Based Initial Teacher Training (ITT) Mentors*. Available at https://assets.publishing. service.gov.uk/government/uploads/system/uploads/attachment_data/file/536891/Mentor_standards_report_Final.pdf (accessed 17 April 2019).

Thomas, W. and Smith, A. (2009) *Coaching Solutions: Practical Ways to Improve Performance in Education*. London: Network Continuum.

VIA Institute on Character (2019). *The VIA Survey*. Available at https://www.viacharacter.org/www/Character-Strengths-Survey (accessed 16 April 2019).

Whitmore, J. (1992) *Coaching for Performance*. London: Nicholas Brealey.

Wilson, P. and Long, I. (2015) *The Blob School*. London: Routledge.

Zenger, J. and Stinnett, K. (2010) *The Extraordinary Coach: How the Best Leaders Help Others Grow*. New York: McGraw-Hill Education.

8

CONCLUSION

CHAPTER OBJECTIVES

By the end of this chapter you should be aware of:

- the need for high-quality school mentors for trainees and early career teachers
- the factors that should be promoted by effective mentoring
- the role of mentoring as part of a whole school process
- the role that mentoring plays in developing and establishing outstanding pedagogical and professional practice in trainee and early career teachers
- the need for an effective partnership between mentors, ITT institutions, trainees and their training institutions.

INTRODUCTION

This chapter provides an opportunity to critically reflect on how this book may have enhanced your ability as an effective mentor. It will provide an opportunity to consider the key factors of mentoring including developing positive relationships, working in effective partnerships, promoting pedagogical knowledge and promoting professionalism. It will seek to show the incremental role you will play in developing critically reflective and independent practitioners and how, by engaging in mentoring, you may also develop your own practice and have the ability to act as research-informed practitioner.

THE ROLE OF MENTORING

As a mentor, your role and commitment to supporting and enhancing the pool of future talented trainee and early career teachers will be of paramount importance.

There can be no question, having read this book, that mentoring must be seen as a 'dynamic process' (Gardiner and Weisling, 2018, p.331) which is multifaceted given the complexity of the knowledge, skills and attitudes needed to undertake such a position. As shown in Figure 8.1, key factors to being an effective mentor include developing positive relationships, working in effective partnerships, promoting pedagogical knowledge and promoting professionalism.

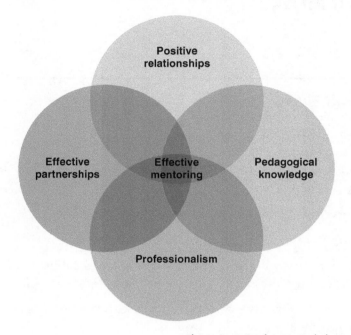

Figure 8.1   Key factors to being an effective mentor

For some teachers, this role will be new and, as discussed in Chapter 1, your selection for this role may be based upon a chance professional conversation or a personal desire to help the next generation of teachers. What can be in no doubt is that for many of you, as mentors, your role will have evolved over time, you will have learned on the job and many of the keys skills, concepts and techniques of mentoring – as outlined in Chapter 7 – may have evolved with little training, unless provided through the support of your school and university-based partnership(s).

As this book has suggested, the mentoring of trainee and early career teachers will inevitably involve factors such as establishing relationships, sharing ideas and pedagogical knowledge, as well as developing a shared understanding of the professional role (Aderibigbe et al., 2018). It will also mean providing structured support to build on students' knowledge and experience (Estyn, 2018; DfE, 2019). So, importantly, what can you do to ensure that your mentoring of trainees and early career teachers is successful?

DEVELOP POSiTiVE RELATiONSHiPS

From the outset, make certain each individual you mentor feels that they belong. Try, as Shields and Murray (2017) found in their study, to avoid being a mentor who has been given a trainee and is resentful about this. Try to avoid thinking of the extra work that your mentee will generate, which might manifest in you having 'little time for them' (Estyn, 2018, p.12). Whatever the circumstance, try to make your trainee feel welcome and that they belong in this new professional community. As Shields and Murray (2017, p.7) suggest, 'belonging support' involves trainees feeling accepted into their new environment. They go on to rightly note that the Mentor Standards (Teaching Schools Council, 2016) do not talk directly about belonging, but it is implicit within them. For the Mentor Standards, trust, empathy, integrity, honesty and respect are key in a relationship (Teaching Schools Council, 2016) as outlined in Chapter 2.

Such a strong, open and honest mentor/mentee relationship is not only important in the short term for a trainee, but will also influence teacher identity (Izadinia, 2016). Strong enduring relationships will also be pivotal in supporting the mental health and well-being of your mentee (Howard et al. 2019) given the stresses and strains they will face being new to the profession. Remember to consider how your own values and attitudes may hinder you from forging, or even help you to forge, stronger empathetic relationships. As with the Mentor Standards (Teaching Schools Council, 2016), it is important that you offer integrity and an attitude of 'being in it together' (Shields and Murray, 2017, p.325) to get the best out of your relationship with your mentee. An open and honest relationship, built on trust, will allow your mentees to question and reflect upon their own emerging practice, though in the end it will be up to you to decide how much support is needed. It is also important to remember that a mentoring relationship can also support the mentee's well-being (Estyn, 2018). Try recalling the start of your teaching career, how vulnerable you may have felt or even underprepared for a teaching role and how stressful being new was. Remember that an investment of emotional support can make a daily difference to a mentee's self-efficacy. As Shields and Murray suggest:

> beginning teachers perceived the most effective mentors as the ones who 'go beyond' pedagogical support and are also able to offer emotional support as well as allow them the freedom to try new ideas. (Shields and Murray, 2017, p.328)

Having said all this, it is also important to acknowledge that relationships will not be easy given the balance you have to maintain when combining support for mentees (this may include social, personal and professional support) with your role involving accountability and their assessment (O'Sullivan and Conway, 2016).

Given the complex nature of the demands placed on mentors, such a role might at times feel a burden or yet another item to fit into your school day. However, it is important that you acknowledge that your role as mentor can bring many positive professional and personal benefits. These may include, for example, learning new professional perspectives and current knowledge relating to teaching (Aspfors and Fransson, 2015), as well as experimenting and allowing yourself to become more calculated in your approach to teaching (Bressman et al., 2018). You may also learn to reflect more on the role that your emotional intelligence can play in your ability to, for example, empathise with others. Engaging in the mentoring process will provide you and your mentee with an opportunity to critically reflect on and re-evaluate your and others' current practice. As Tonna et al. (2017) crucially indicate, reflection is the means by which teacher independence of thought may be promoted. It can also provide individuals with an opportunity to challenge their own currently held norms and practice with regards to being a teaching professional.

BUILDING EFFECTIVE PARTNERSHIPS

The partnership(s) with your university-based colleagues/organisation(s) will enable you to promote outstanding mentoring (as discussed in Chapter 5). Remember, though, you may have a daily responsibility to your trainee and eventually will have to assess their standard of practice – it will be your university partners who award QTS status.

As the Mentor Standards (Teaching Schools Council, 2016, p.8) suggest, effective high-quality ITT support involves a:

> systematic process to identify, train and develop school-based ITT mentors to support trainee teachers to develop their teaching practice and retain good teachers in the classroom for as long as possible.

However, despite such laudable sentiments, Estyn (2018) notes one crucial element that needs to be addressed: i.e. the partnership between university and school. By providing insights into the university-based programmes trainees will gain an enhanced ability to connect educational theory to teaching practice.

Part of being a mentor, therefore, must be to establish a good understanding of your role as outlined by your university partners – it must equally include you being a 'teacher educator'. As Estyn (2018, p.6) suggests, this involves you being involved in:

> the pedagogy of ITE ... specifically the approaches that they [mentors] take to teaching students how to teach, including developing subject knowledge and developing pedagogy.

This will inevitably involve your engagement in professional learning activities as well as research, which may include higher level research (Estyn, 2018). As Estyn (2018) rightly points out, such learning may not always seem directly linked to mentoring; it will, however, provide you with transferable, skills such as being reflective. It may also develop aspects of your subject knowledge, and allow your mentee to see you as a professional learner as well.

Though such an idea may seem daunting at first, seek help and advice from your university-based setting as to how you could be involved.

- Try supporting course programmes (this will allow for you to disseminate your own expertise as well as learn about research and ideas currently taught at the university).

- See if you can get involved in, or ask if you can support, a small-scale research project.

- See what further study may be available to you at your university-based partner(s).

As Cain (2009, p.63) suggests, mentors being involved with research can allow for a 'new way of thinking'. This may ultimately, as he suggests, not only allow for an enhanced understanding of a mentor's own professional practice but also of the associated research literature.

PEDAGOGICAL AND PROFESSIONAL KNOWLEDGE

As a mentor, your role will be key in developing a trainee's pedagogical knowledge (as discussed in Chapter 3), with such a concept inevitably including the promotion of professionalism in your mentee (as outlined in Chapter 4). By developing professionalism in your trainees, you are allowing them to participate in/understand the life of the school and its role within the wider community. It will also include supporting a trainee's professional and personal conduct with items such as the need to promote equality, diversity and safeguarding (Teaching Schools Council, 2016).

As with professionalism, good practice will involve you as a mentor in the development of aspects of practice along with the incremental acquisition of pedagogical knowledge. In the beginning, structured scaffolded learning will provide the key to effective mentoring. It is important, however, as Shields and Murray (2017, p.327) suggest, that you allow 'space' for your mentees to try out new things whilst allowing them a sense of 'ownership of activities'. As trainees develop, such structured support may then develop into increasing levels of independence, reflection and criticality (Estyn, 2018).

As discussed in Chapter 2, it is important that you encourage the trainee to reflect on their practice, with you as their mentor providing a means by which a trainee may see the modelling of outstanding practice across aspects of teaching and learning. Such experiences may be enhanced by the use of video analysis (as outlined in Chapter 3) or by example, allowing a trainee to observe your and others' lessons/professional practice. Effective pedagogical knowledge may also be developed through the use of accurate written feedback that captures a student's progress and the setting of specific targets, as well as learning conversations and dialogue between you and your mentee (Estyn, 2018). As Jones et al. (2019, p.131) note, this may require you to review the time, space and regular use of two-way dialogue with your mentee as well as how you foster trusting and reciprocal relationships.

By the use of skilful mentoring, the practice outlined above will allow you to develop a mentee's ability to be critical and reflective. It will also be fundamentally important if you are to help trainees to analyse their practice and see the links that can be made with the educational theories instilled through their university-based programmes of study.

CONCLUDING REMARKS

To finish, it is also important for you to realise, however daunting all the above may seem, that your position as a mentor should not be a role or burden you must carry alone. As Estyn (2018, p.6) notes:

> the most effective mentoring takes place in schools where there is an established culture of learning. In these schools, there is a strong focus on developing effective teaching. Supporting student teachers to improve their skills, knowledge and understanding is seen as part of a continuum of professional learning.

Given this, it is important for you to reflect upon the following questions to end this chapter.

KEY REFLECTIONS

- Does your school promote a culture which values learning?
- How are you trained and supported in your role to help mentees to develop their skills and their knowledge of teaching?
- Does your role involve high-quality support from your university provider?

- How might you effectively engage in school/university-based partnerships?
- How might you engage in further training/research as a teacher educator?
- How do you think your future role as a mentor can, and should, develop?

SUGGESTED FURTHER READING

Cain, T. (2009) Mentoring trainee teachers: how can mentors use research? *Mentoring and Tutoring: Partnership in Learning*, 17(1), 53–66.

Jones, L., Tones, S., and Foulkes, G. (2018) Mentoring associate teachers in initial teacher education: the value of dialogic feedback. *International Journal of Mentoring and Coaching in Education*, 7(2), 127–38. Available at https://doi.org/10.1108/IJMCE-07-2017-0051

Jones, L., Tones, S. and Foulkes, G. (2019) Exploring learning conversations between mentors and associate teachers in initial teacher education. *International Journal of Mentoring and Coaching in Education*. 8(2), 120–33. Available at https://www.emerald.com/insight/content/doi/10.1108/IJMCE-08-2018-0050/full/html (accessed 11 July 2019).

Shields, S. and Murray, M. (2017) Beginning teachers' perceptions of mentors and access to communities of practice. *International Journal of Mentoring and Coaching in Education*, 6(4), 317–31.

Tonna, M.A., Bjerkholt, E. and Holland, E. (2017) Teacher mentoring and the reflective practitioner approach. *International Journal of Mentoring and Coaching in Education*, 6(3), 210–27.

REFERENCES

Aderibigbe, S., Graye, D.S. and Colucci-Gray, L. (2018) Understanding the nature of mentoring experiences between teachers and student teachers. *International Journal of Mentoring and Coaching in Education*, 7(1), 54–71.

Aspfors, J. and Fransson, G. (2015) Research on mentor education for mentors of newly qualified teachers: a qualitative meta-synthesis. *Teaching and Teacher Education*, 48, 75–86.

Bressman, S., Winter, J.S. and Efron, S.E. (2018) Next generation mentoring: supporting teachers beyond induction. *Teaching and Teacher Education*, 73, 162–70.

Cain, T. (2009) Mentoring trainee teachers: how can mentors use research? *Mentoring and Tutoring: Partnership in Learning*, 17(1), 53–66.

Department for Education (DfE) (2019) *Early Career Framework*. Available at https://assets.publishing.service.gov.uk/government/uploads/system/uploads/attachment_data/file/773705/Early-Career_Framework.pdf (accessed 4 April 2019).

Estyn (2018) The professional learning continuum: mentoring in initial teacher education. Available at https://www.estyn.gov.wales/sites/www.estyn.gov.wales/files/documents/Mentoring%20in%20initial%20teacher%20education%20-%20en.pdf (accessed 5 July 2019).

Gardiner, W. and Weisling, N. (2018) Challenges and complexities of developing mentors' practice: insights from new mentors. *International Journal of Mentoring and Coaching in Education*, 7(4), 329–432.

Hobson, A.J. and Malderez, A. (2013) Judgementoring and other threats to realizing the potential of school-based mentoring in teacher education. *International Journal of Mentoring and Coaching in Education*, 2(2), 89–108.

Howard, C., Burton, M. and Levermore, D. (2019) *Children's Mental Health and Emotional Well-being in Primary Schools* (2nd edn). London: SAGE.

Izadinia, M. (2016) Student teachers' and mentor-teachers' perceptions and expectations of a mentoring relationship: do they match or clash? *Professional Development in Education*, 42(3), 387–402.

Jones, L., Tones, S. and Foulkes, G. (2019) Exploring learning conversations between mentors and associate teachers in initial teacher education. *International Journal of Mentoring and Coaching in Education*. 8(2), 120–33. Available at https://www.emerald.com/insight/content/doi/10.1108/IJMCE-08-2018-0050/full/html (accessed 11 July 2019).

O'Sullivan, D. and Conway, P.F. (2016) Underwhelmed and playing it safe: newly qualified primary teachers' mentoring and probationary-related experiences during induction. *Irish Educational Studies*, 35(4), 403–20.

Shields, S. and Murray, M. (2017) Beginning teachers' perceptions of mentors and access to communities of practice. *International Journal of Mentoring and Coaching in Education*, 6(4), 317–31.

Tonna, M.A., Bjerkholt, E. and Holland, E. (2017) Teacher mentoring and the reflective practitioner approach. *International Journal of Mentoring and Coaching in Education*, 6(3), 210–27.

APPENDIX
SELF-AUDIT ANSWERS

CHAPTER 1. THE PROFESSIONAL ROLE OF A TEACHER MENTOR

Q. How would you define mentoring?

The definition of mentoring is open to interpretation given the breadth of its role. However its definition centres on an organised and ongoing process to support trainees to gain QTS, as well as supporting early career teachers to successfully pass their induction period so as to become outstanding professionals. Mentoring involves a long-term developmental relationship with a more senior/experienced teacher who can offer mentees guidance and support both personally and professionally to support their career and its progression.

Q. Why is a successful partnership needed to support mentoring in schools?

Mentoring forms part of a valued partnership between ITT providers and that of school-based colleagues/settings. By both organisations working together and by them having a clear knowledge/expectations of trainee's or early career teacher's developmental needs this partnership can provide a positive climate which will enable individuals to achieve professional expectations.

Q. Why is effective mentoring important for trainee teachers and early career teachers?

Given that individuals will find the task of obtaining QTS and providing outstanding teaching and learning difficult at times, effective mentoring can help support trainees and early career teachers with the knowledge, skills and attitudes needed to be successful.

Q. What are the skills, attitudes and areas of knowledge needed by outstanding school mentors?

The range of skills, attitudes and knowledge needed to be outstanding as mentor are immense. Critically they will involve items such as:

- personal organisation, attention to detail, be able to model outstanding practice

- a knowledge of what outstanding teaching involves and looks like

- an understanding of what is required to obtain QTS, to meet the Teachers' Standards and what is needed to successfully pass induction

- interpersonal skills such as being able to show empathy, to be receptive and reflective when challenged, to be trustworthy and to be a good listener.

Q. Why is there a need for a set of National Mentor Standards?

National Mentor Standards are needed to provide clarity, equity and coherence to what is an important aspect of trainee teachers and early career teachers training. Such standards may provide a means to establish a greater status and recognition of this role in a trainee and teaching professional's development.

CHAPTER 2. STANDARD 1: PERSONAL QUALITIES

Q. What do you understand by the term 'empathy', and how might you have shown this in your mentoring?

Empathy will be a key factor in your ability to develop positive relationships with your mentee. It will enable you to a large extent to appreciate and understand the feelings of others. Empathy will allow you to be emotionally self-aware which will let you more effectively listen to and communicate with your trainee or early career teacher regarding their professional development. Empathy will no doubt be easy with mentees when you think about your early career and the struggles you faced. Though things may have changed professionally in the demands made on early career teachers and trainees some items will not have changed significantly – for example, what is like to hold your first parents' evening. These are the things you may most easily empathise with.

Q. What do you understand by the term 'trust', and how might you have shown this in your mentoring?

Trust, as with empathy, will involve the use of emotional intelligence. It will also be built on a mutually agreeable relationship where the trainee or early career teacher knows you can be relied upon to be open to worries and to be honest. Trust may involve, if appropriate, confidentiality or a non-judgemental approach to conversations. At times it will involve you being a critical friend where sometimes unpalatable hard truths can be shared. It is important to realise, however, that trust will not always be easy to secure given that there is an element of the mentee feeling that, at the end of it all, you will assess their progress. This may make them reluctant to share some of their professional worries. Trust may take different forms in your ongoing professional relationship with your mentee. This can, for example, be seen through you, as the mentor, allowing mentees autonomy in terms of how they dismiss the class or respond when dealing with an upset parent.

Q. What do you understand by the term 'modelling of practice', and how might you have shown this in your mentoring?

Modelling of practice will allow a mentee to observe your and other professional pedagogical practice. It may take the form of your mentee observing a specific lesson or aspect of a lesson through clear lesson foci. Such practice may allow the trainee or early career teacher to reflect on their own professional practice as well as giving them the opportunity to discuss and review elements of practice. To ensure this strategy's success make certain you have set clear ground rules, have allocated quality time for feedback and find a place where you are happy to discuss things and will not be interrupted.

Q. What are the skills and attitudes needed to promote empathy and trust between mentor and mentee?

To secure empathy and trust you must be someone who can be relied on to keep their word (if there is no conflict of professionalism, e.g. safeguarding issues). You must be a good listener who can use your emotional intelligent effectively to promote a positive outcome to items. You must try not to be judgemental as well as being open and honest in your discussions. You should not mix sympathy up with the notion of empathy and you must try and avoid your own values and attitudes clouding your relationship with a mentee.

Q. Why are trust, empathy and modelling vital to securing outstanding trainee/early career practice?

By showing high levels of trust and empathy you will ensure, through being a critical friend, that your mentee can review and reflect upon their professional practice. It will allow them to move towards what they may consider to be their ideal self, as well as aligning their own practice more closely to the characteristics of outstanding practice.

CHAPTER 3. STANDARD 2: TEACHING

Q. How might you further develop your ability to frame language to impact positively upon a coaching conversation?

It is difficult to self-assess how we ourselves use language within a coaching conversation, so you may initially want to consider one of two approaches. Firstly, you might facilitate an observation of yourself whilst in 'coaching mode'. This could be 'live' or via recorded means – in which case ensure you get the permission of the other colleague that is being recorded. The advantage to recording your discussions is that you can watch yourself whilst sharing your thoughts and reflections with an appropriate colleague. The ability to 'pause' and 'replay' also enables you to revisit the session and build on previous reflections once you become more adept at your use of language and self-reflection. Alternatively, you might consider careful planning of the language that you intend to use, almost initially like a 'script'. For less confident mentors this might be a good place to start. You will refine and develop your language choices and structure as you become more confident and competent. You might of course use a combination of both strategies if you have the capacity and relevant support.

Q. How might you manage your limited time for mentoring support to enable your mentee to have the best possible opportunity for discussion and reflection?

Firstly, make sure that the time and place are right for a fruitful discussion. The staffroom at 6pm on a Friday afternoon before the half term break will not be the most effective time for discussion so be kind to yourselves and manage the basics well! In order to make the best possible use of the discussion time that you have, it is also wise to agree on what you and your mentee want to discuss before you actually meet. This 'mini agenda' enables both of you to come to the meeting prepared to explore the focus areas and to bring with you the relevant evidence/resources to support an active discussion, e.g. children's books, journal reflections, videoed lesson observation. It is vital to make sure that you do not try to manage a huge agenda within a limited time frame. Be realistic about what you can achieve and make sure that you carefully but briefly record any actions for either of you before you leave. Do not forget to put a date in the diary for the next meeting so that you can follow up anything that you want to develop.

CHAPTER 4. STANDARD 3: PROFESSIONALISM

Q. What does professionalism look like in your mentor role?

You will now be familiar with how professionalism is understood. Integral to being a professional is having knowledge and expertise to link theory and practice. A key skill is helping others to find solutions. A professional is a good role model to others, manages their own feelings, builds positive working relationships, develops trust and treats everyone equally and without discrimination, all of which are essential traits.

Q. How can young teachers be supported to stay in the teaching profession?

Two areas of concern have been highlighted in teacher retention: managing workload and maintaining a work–life balance. You can help by ensuring there is good communication with the new teacher, that there is support so that they feel empowered and responsible alongside considering how the work environment recognises and rewards these teachers to stay passionate about teaching.

Q. What strategies do you have to manage a healthy balance between your personal and professional life?

Never give up your passions. Dedicate 'me' time so that you are healthy and well for others. Although the school day is a busy one, find time in it to step away for at least ten minutes. Take a walk, meditate, be alone, read a magazine – whatever helps you to reconnect. Ensure you have someone who you can talk to. Take time in your personal life to immerse yourself in something that makes you feel happy.

Q. How do you keep up to date with your professional development needs?

Alongside your annual review with senior leaders, there are many opportunities to for CPD. Engage in scholarly reading, write an article for a curriculum subject journal, such as *Primary Geography*, attend or contribute to a conference, join a forum, write a blog, work with the local university to lead a workshop, read the *Times Educational Supplement* or *Education Guardian* to keep up to date.

Q. What support can you give to new teachers to feel confident in working with parents/carers?

Your experience in dealing with a range of situations will be invaluable here. Listen to the teacher's concerns and provide useful strategies such as using role play to enact situations, develop a bank of useful phrases to draw upon, learn how to actively listen, attend a parent/carer consultation and give feedback to the new teacher. Encourage the teacher to talk to other teachers who know the families and create informal opportunities to talk to parents/carers.

CHAPTER 5. STANDARD 4: SELF-DEVELOPMENT AND WORKING IN PARTNERSHIP

Q. How might you ensure that your mentoring judgements and working routines align with best practice?

It is important to ensure that you prioritise your own professional development. You will be a more effective mentor if you constantly reflect on your own professional needs, rather than purely those of your mentee. Start with an audit of your areas of strength and those areas that require further development. You might use the *National Standards for School-Based Initial Teacher Training (ITT)*

Mentors (Teaching Schools Council, 2016, available at https://assets.publishing. service.gov.uk/government/uploads/system/uploads/attachment_data/file/536891/ Mentor_standards_report_Final.pdf) as a starting point; it would be wise to make this a collaborative process alongside your own mentor/appraiser. Plan a range of formal and informal opportunities which you are able to access over the course of the year, e.g. mentor training provided by your HEI partnership, shadowing a more experienced mentor, accessing resources from the Research and Practice Centre 'CollectivED: The Mentoring and Coaching Hub' (Leeds Beckett University Carnegie School of Education, various dates, available at https://www.leedsbeckett. ac.uk/carnegie-school-of-education/research/working-paper-series/collectived/), enabling the development of a community of mentors within your school. Throughout the year, revisit your initial audit and gauge whether you are making progress towards your own professional development goals.

Q. How might you further develop your research knowledge? What resources could you seek out and who might you share this knowledge with?

Firstly, consider which 'research knowledge' focus would align with your professional development needs. You might refer to your own skills audit here to give you a steer.

Next, consider what avenues of research support you currently have access to, e.g. a university partnership, a local research school, a colleague in school who values a research-informed approach, a professional Twitter account, membership of the Chartered College of Teaching. Protect a little time each week to explore a research article and share this with a colleague or your own mentee. You might even put a copy on the staffroom noticeboard to find out which colleagues might be interested in collaborating with you. Reflect on whether the article has research credibility and how you might (or indeed might not) utilise any of your reflections to develop your own pedagogy. Ensure that you glean support throughout from your own mentor/appraiser.

CHAPTER 6. PROFESSIONAL MENTORING SKILLS

Q. Which mentoring skills were covered within this chapter?

- Contracting
- Building rapport
- Active listening
- Questioning

- Summarising

- Challenging

- Giving feedback

Q. Which of these skills creates the basis for all future mentoring discussions with a mentee?

Contracting. Conducting a contracting discussion with your mentee, at the very start of your mentoring relationship, will help ensure that you are both clear about your joint expectations and your individual responsibilities. It also needs to include a discussion about confidentiality, i.e. what information will remain between the two of you and what will be passed onto others.

Q. Who created the Spectrum of Coaching model included in this chapter?

The Spectrum of Coaching model, included in this chapter, was created by Myles Downey. It was included in his book entitled *Effective Coaching*, published in 1999, and more recently within *Effective Modern Coaching*, published in 2014 (both London: LID).

Q. When asking an open question, which word do we suggest you avoid starting a question with and for what reasons?

Whilst it is common, in general conversation, to start an open question with 'Why' there are many authors – including Downey (2014), Thomas and Smith (2009), Whitmore (2009) and Davies (2016) (see Chapter 6 for reference details) – who advise against its use. This is because starting a question with 'Why' can create defensiveness in a mentee and encourage them to come up with excuses rather than a considered response.

CHAPTER 7. MODELS AND TECHNIQUES FOR MENTORING

Q. What benefits can result from a mentor's use of models and techniques as part of their mentoring approach?

Using a process model can help you to structure your mentoring discussions. Keeping the model in mind will help you to support your mentee in their identification of a goal, encourage them to explore their current situation, generate the options open to them and then plan their next steps.

Using techniques, when appropriate, as part of your mentoring approach can help your mentee to reflect upon a situation they are in, to gain new insights and to identify what their next steps could be.

Q. Name the reflective practice model covered within this chapter.

The reflective practice model contained within this chapter is Gibbs' six-stage reflective model (1988, *Learning by Doing*. Oxford: Oxford Further Education Unit). It was initially developed for teachers, and can help your mentees to learn from situations they face on a regular basis.

Q. Name three of the therapeutic approaches that models and techniques within this chapter have emerged from.

- Positive psychology
- Motivational interviewing
- Gestalt

Q. Which technique, mentioned within this chapter, was developed as part of the Gestalt approach?

The Empty Chair technique has its origins in the Gestalt approach. This technique can be particularly helpful when you would like your mentee to consider another person's view of the situation they are talking about. It can sometimes help the mentee to be more objective and to gain some additional insights into how their own thoughts and behaviour may be affecting the relationship.

iNDEX